THE HERO OF TIGER HILL

THE HERO OF TIGER HILL

Autobiography of a Param Vir

Capt (Hony)
YOGENDRA SINGH YADAV

An imprint of
Srishti Publishers & Distributors

Srishti Publishers & Distributors
A unit of AJR Publishing LLP
212A, Peacock Lane
Shahpur Jat, New Delhi – 110 049
editorial@srishtipublishers.com

First published by Bold,
an imprint of Srishti Publishers & Distributors in 2022

Copyright © Capt Yogendra Singh Yadav, 2022

10 9 8 7 6 5 4 3 2 1

This is a work of non-fiction based on the author's life and experiences in the Indian Army. While due care has been taken by the author and publisher to verify content at press time, any inadvertent miss that is brought to their notice shall be duly verified and updated subsequently. Actual names of people and places have been used with a view to provide first-hand information.

The author asserts the moral right to be identified as the author of this work.

All rights reserved. No part of this publication may be reproduced, stored in a retrieval system, or transmitted, in any form or by any means, electronic, mechanical, photocopying, recording or otherwise, without the prior written permission of the Publishers.

Printed and bound in India

A note from the author

I have been extremely lucky to have met and be supported by all the right people in this lifetime. I wouldn't be here, if not for the support of my loved ones, friends and associates.

I am forever thankful to god for granting me this life. My mother, Smt Santara Devi and father, Sh Ramkaran Singh Yadav, always encouraged me to be a good person. It is their teachings and constant motivation that instilled confidence in me from a young age.

My heartfelt thanks to the Indian Army for showing me what it is to live and die for the nation. Gratitude to ADG PI for their support and guidance in bringing this book to you.

I thank all my fellows, jawans and officers at 18 Grenadiers for their love and support in the happiest and toughest of times.

And special thanks to all those dear friends who motivated me to write my life experiences in a book and kept me going.

I hope you enjoy reading my varied life experiences and the most pivotal event that changed my life forever.

Jai Hind!

Yogendra Singh Yadav
August 2022

Prologue

I was walking slowly along with my team, carefully scanning the entire area. The enemy could be anywhere. Who knew which rock could turn out to be the last one we crossed, or where the enemy sat, ready to pounce upon us. So we treaded carefully at every step.

We had not gone far when we started getting out of breath. The lack of oxygen at this altitude was crippling for the best of us. So we moved bit by bit, resting every now and then to catch our breath and stabilize our bodies.

In a few minutes, we came upon a cliff which seemed impossible to climb. It was imperative for us to go to the other side if we wished to reach Tiger Hill. We threw a rope up and it got stuck somewhere. Then we climbed up the rock, uphill along the steep climb, with the help of that rope. I was the first to pull myself on top of the cliff. Once there, I looked around, ensuring clear ground around me and carefully tied the rope to a cliff. Then the other *jawans* climbed up, helping each other.

The little sound made by our feet touching the rock and dislodging a few small stones in the process was rather loud in the deathly silent night. As the stones fell, they also made a piercing sound. At night when it is quiet all around, even a low sound sounds like a loud one.

I noticed that the sky had started getting lighter and guessed it was close to dawn. All of a sudden, the soldiers from the Pakistani bunkers on both sides of the cliff started firing at us. By that time, just about seven of us had managed to climb up. The rest were curtailed due to the heavy firing from both the sides.

Our route was now cut off. The rest of the party was unable to climb up. And those of us who were up there already, were unable to go either left or right. The seven of us climbed up further ahead and saw a large plain area. There were two bunkers right in front of us.

We took position and started firing. Within moments, we had managed to kill the Pakistani soldiers in those bunkers in direct, face to face firing. We could finally see the Tiger Hill ahead of us.

That plain was the enemy's point of defense. In our quick recce of the area, we could estimate about a hundred and fifty Pakistani soldiers stationed around us. When they heard the sound of our firing, they also started firing at us very heavily.

Indian soldiers are not taught to step back, and in the given situation, moving forward meant sure death. We were surrounded on all sides. In such a situation, when death seems to be the only option, fear vanishes. After all, we were soldiers who had been living in the midst of heavy firing for quite some time now.

I was not afraid of death. All I prayed for now was to not die before winning back Tiger Hill.

PART – I

FORMATIVE YEARS

1

Childhood Days

There is a village in the Chaubisa region of the district of Bulandshahr called Aurangabad Ahir. Ramkaran used to farm his land and his wife Santara Devi helped in every possible way. They had a small family that worked hard tilling their land, giving their children the best possible facilities. I was born in this family on 10 May 1980.

I have grown up admiring my two brothers and father for their incredible qualities. My elder brother Jitendra Singh has been my idol ever since I started understanding the society around me. Devendra Singh is the younger one, who I love rather fondly. Our father is an ex-serviceman[1] and our mother, a homemaker. Our parents raised us very well using what they earned by farming.

---

1. As part of the Kumaon Regiment, he also participated in the 1965 and 1971 Indo-Pak wars.

The three of us have seen our parents working extremely hard all through the year. Even when my father was away on duty, we would see him come back home on leave and spend most of his time tilling the land or harvesting the crops. In fact, he timed his leave as per the crop cycles to ensure that we got the best possible harvest.

So from a very young age, we helped our parents in all their work. In this way, we learned to do things together and made sure we had a comfortable life. The atmosphere at home was mostly jovial as, along with work, we had a good time. We were known as the 'happy lot' all across the village. Along with a supportive family, we also had a bunch of loyal and loving friends.

I think such brotherhood and camaraderie has become a luxury these days as people are more need-driven and self-oriented. However, this was part and parcel of life in the village as the strong sense of community is entrenched in its inherent culture.

If you enter a village even today, you will see people sitting in groups, talking for hours, often bursting into loud laughter just as suddenly.

Evenings in villages are the perfect time to talk about what happened during the day while puffing at the *hookah,* going back to the days of childhood, discussing matters related to their homes, society and the country in general. Days started really early and time flew. The day was over before we even knew it.

Honestly speaking, back in our village, the elderly sit together and talk in this way even now. They gather around by evening and share their thoughts and experiences with each other. This is the best way to instill a feeling of fellowship in the community. Not only that, it helps the young people to learn a lot from what their elders have to say. Unfortunately, I haven't seen this kind of practice in cities. I find this to be a good way to unwind, getting rid of their tension and physical exhaustion.

When they laugh out loud, it refreshes their bodies and minds. This activity is essential for physical fitness, which is why they do not fall ill very often. Even the women wake up at 4 a.m. and get busy, tending to their cattle, giving them fodder From an early age, we getting on with other household work. They help menfolk in the fields after that, working shoulder to shoulder. Along with all this, they look after their children.

That is the kind of environment I grew up in. This is how I perceived my world when I first opened my eyes. And this is how I learnt some of the most precious life lessons.

From an early age, we saw that our mother would wake up at 4 every morning, give fodder to the cattle, collect cow dung and clean the cattle shed. Then she would light the *chulha,* prepare tea for all of us and make us sit and study. She would sit next to us, cooking on the open stove after milking the buffaloes. My father or elder brother took the milk to the cooperative milk dairy.

I used to be astonished at how my mother finished cooking as well as cleaning the whole house before 7 a.m. each day. By 7.30 a.m., after sending us to school, our parents sat on the bullock cart and left to work in the fields. We did not have a lot of land, but whatever we had, the produce from it sufficed to fulfill our needs.

Little did I know that this hard work, discipline and the tendency to utilize the available time in the best way would come in so handy in my life as a soldier. I guess the preparation had begun from early on in life, the result of which is for all of us to see.

My brother and I watched our parents doing their work very diligently and meticulously – how they completed more work in a short time and in an effective way. This was true in every household in the village. Everyone worked hard during the day and sat together in the evening to share their stories.

Tobacco and *hookah* were popular in these evening group activities. The elders sat together and puffed at the hookah, including Maa and her friends, who discussed their day, including their children's studies, farming and what was happening in the country in general.

To this day, people finish their dinner by six or seven in the evening and go to sleep by nine in most villages, except those who are busy with their hookah.

In our house too, the hookah smokers sat for their session every night. Most of the members of the group were my father's childhood friends and a few young men of the locality. I had no choice but to be a part of the group as my cot was close to where they sat. Plus, it used to be my duty to refill the *chillum* as and when needed. Papa had given me the responsibility of keeping a low fire ready with the help of dung cakes for this purpose. So I had to remain awake for this. Sometimes I would study, however most of the time, I would listen to what was being discussed. It was the same routine every day.

Now I realize how much I learnt just by listening to those people. Since that was their time to talk about various issues freely, it served as an excellent learning point for me. At times I learnt from what they did in their daily lives as well. Whatever the source might be, these things laid a strong foundation in our lives.

> *Those who have it in them to face struggle and challenges, are better prepared for success.*

2

The First Lessons

Won't you agree that home is the first learning place for the child? All those who are elder to us act like teachers and guide us using their knowledge and experience. There is no blackboard at home, no notebook, no pen or pencil, but something new can be learnt at every step of the way. Maybe at that time, we fail to understand this because we are too young and naïve.

But when we grow up a little and become sensible, it becomes crystal clear that what our parents taught prepared us to live life in a far better way than what we managed to learn from our books. We realize this when we praise those who are able to lead a successful life.

I remember when papa sat with us for dinner every night, he would talk about his defining life incidents. He would explain various problems and how he tackled them. Like Abhimanyu following Arjun's words to crack the *chakravyuha,* his words prepped us for any challenge that could stop us.

He often told us about how people take advantage of our weakness. He would often tell us that we need to keep an eye on our goal. Then, he would summarize, 'When you become successful, people will treat you with a lot of respect. This would add to your status and make you more honourable.' His words seem to have come true.

If I take my own example, I see how a number of people link their name with mine with pride. We are looked up to as a family that has served the nation. Both my brothers are leading respectable lives too – one is a Subedar in the Army, while the other works in a private office.

On the other hand are those who have not been as successful because they are treading the wrong path. They are not only boycotted by the society, but also that nobody – including their closest kin – wants to link their names with such people. I can comprehend these things clearly now and remember how our father would enlighten us on these truths of life casually over a meal. He would say, 'The roti that satisfies your hunger doesn't just come to your plate. The farmer works on his fields day and night, putting in all his energy. Leaves no stone unturned to look after the crop. You should be thankful for it.'

There were times when we did not like him being away at odd hours to check on the crop. We would ask him to relax for a bit. But he used to say with a smile, 'You say there is nothing to be done in the fields, and still I go there! You ask me why I keep taking rounds of the field. My son, when you have sown something with so much of love, you will not get rich returns if you do not take good care of it. The field and the crop also notice how much the farmer loves them. It is this mutual attachment that makes them yield a rich harvest.'

You can call it a casual remark, more emotional than practical. But my heart tells me that there is truth in it. Whatever work you are doing, if you just watch over it every day by taking a look at all your resources, a mutual love automatically develops. This is the same degree of affection that grows in a child for the mother who breastfeeds it many times in a day. The child starts crying when someone else picks it up, because it can sense that it isn't the mother. In the same way, the fields also feel for the person who ardently works there every day. I have seen and felt that the fields yield a richer harvest for someone who goes there every day and watches over them, as opposed to those where the landowner goes once in a while. The same is the case with cattle. The home where the cattle is looked after well, always flourishes.

Maybe these small instances taught me to be devoted to my work with all my heart. Not just this, it was after observing this kind of attitude in my father that I sculpted my personality as I grew up. An essential part of it was respecting others, especially women. This important lesson was instilled into my conscience as much by his words as by my own experiences of seeing my mother.

Our father often said, 'Your Maa works day and night and looks after all of you. Care for her and look after her well. A woman is the Lakshmi of the house. A home where women are not respected is never prosperous. It is ultimately ruined because goddess Lakshmi never visits there.'

He taught us to never disrespect women or even think of showing any aggression or violence. He ingrained in us that those who raise their hand on others without reason are cowards. He said something which I remember and abide by, even today. 'The home where there is peace and mutual love among all, always prospers. Just a house built of bricks cannot be called a home. Even if it is just a thatched roof, the mutual affection of all who live there gives it the sanctity of a temple. If people live together with mutual love, live a life that is filled with self satisfaction and happiness, even a thatched hut can be a more grand place than a palace.

These are the truths of life, including some very bitter ones, that only our parents can teach us. Such knowledge cannot be learned from books. That is why I believe that parents are our first teachers and the home is our first school.

> *This life is very precious. We must not waste it away in criticizing others or misusing the power we hold.*

3

Work is Worship

Our family of five lived in a small house in the village. There was just one *pucca* room in which all of us stayed. There were three cots – one for my father, one for my mother and youngest brother, and the third one was shared by me and my elder brother. If a guest or relative came to visit, my brother and I spread a sheaf of paddy on the floor and made our beds on it. While this would look like absolutely no personal space for any of us, this became a blessing in disguise and brought us together.

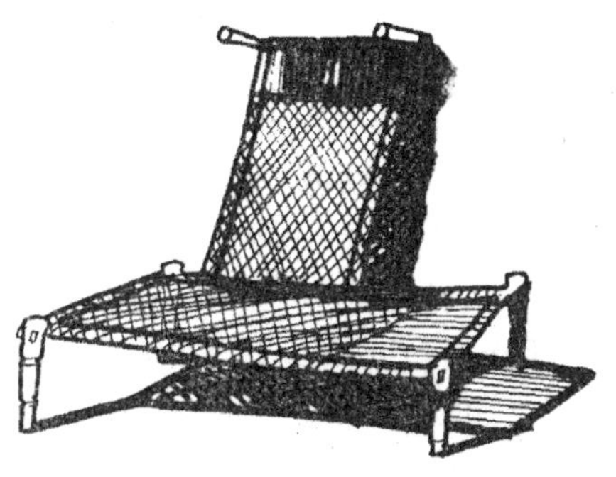

Similarly, whether he was working on the field or taking care of the cattle, our father always took us along. He painstakingly explained the work he was doing. By now, my elder brother had understood the intricacies of almost all the work that was done. I could never fathom why, but Papa seemed to be in a hurry to teach us everything. When other children were still spending time playing around, we learnt as much about most of the work done on the fields and at home.

Not long after, Papa was afflicted by a very serious illness. Back in those days, the hospitals in the district were not so good. The more modern and advanced hospitals were in Delhi or Meerut. We took Papa to all the well-known and respectable doctors in town, but there was no improvement in his health condition. You cannot even imagine the plight of a household where the head of the family is bedridden. All work in the fields came to a halt. For one whole year, our condition was pitiable.

Then one day, our cousin arrived. She had got married to someone in Faridabad in Haryana and my *bua*, my father's sister, lived in the same place. They took Papa with them so that he could receive better medical treatment.

During those days, my mother was in bad shape as she was crying all the time. The whole responsibility of the household had fallen upon her shoulders. She not only took care of us, but also worked in the fields and looked after the cattle. It was too much for her and her health started deteriorating.

It was at this time that our elder brother took it upon himself to shoulder the responsibility of running the household. He was studying in class seven and I was in class four. When my brother ploughed the field with my uncle's help, I would do some of the household work. My mother had divided the work between the two of us. My elder brother worked in the fields and I looked after the cattle. My tasks included bathing them, giving them fodder, cleaning their shed, milking them and taking the milk to the dairy.

One day, I got late in milking the cattle by more than an hour. They started bellowing so loudly that the entire neighborhood would have heard. Actually, I was very fond of playing. I was young and saw my peers having a good time. So, one day, when they asked me to play, I couldn't say no. I got so engrossed in my game that I did not realize how time had flown by and the milking time was long over. I usually gave them fodder, went out to play and came back when it was time to milk them. But that day, I missed it.

Bhaiya and Maa worked in the fields together during that time of the day. When they returned, they heard the buffaloes bellowing. The whole shed was full of their dung. Maa understood what must have happened took charge of the situation. She milked the animals and cleaned up the cattle shed. While things seemed to be under control, both of them were furious!

As soon as I returned home, my elder brother gave me one tight slap and said, 'If you want to help in running the house, you will have to get rid of your childish ways.'

He had said one more thing which I remember even today,

'जो काम बिगाड़े आपनो जग में होत हंसाय
जो काम सुधारे आपनो जग में होत बढ़ाय।'

(One who spoils work given to him, becomes a laughing stock in the world. But the one who puts his own house in order, is praised by all.)

As he explained the profound truth in these lines to me, he added, 'Now see, what you want to do.'

From that day onwards, I decided to abide by what I had learnt from my brother. Even today, it is deeply embedded in my mind. After that day, I had vowed not to go out and play before finishing my work. So while my mother and brother worked in the field, I took on the responsibility of doing all the work around the house.

When everyone does the work assigned to them, no single person feels the brunt of it. In this way, the work gets done in an effective manner. This is the beauty of teamwork. When I joined the Army, I realized it even more deeply.

With some semblance of order and distribution of duties, we managed to send the earnings from farming and milk to my cousin for my father's treatment. The house was also running smoothly.

I learnt from experience that when someone teaches us something, we should try to learn it gradually. It is in this way that nature and one's parents prepare us for the future. The work that feels heavy on your shoulders is actually helping to strengthen your character. Believe me, it is your work that gives you your identity in the long run.

It is only your work that paves the way for your progress and development. The child who forms the habit of working hard from an early age is able to walk the path of life in the best possible manner.

> *All our actions influence others in some way or the other. So do good, be good, and propagate more goodness in the world.*

4

From Bhaiya, with Love

In any home, no matter what the conditions are, the eldest child wields a great influence on the younger children. This might be through the way they behave, the ideas they have or any other activity that distinguishes them. In fact, it is generally said that if the eldest child turns out well, the other siblings follow. There might be some exceptions, but this is generally true.

My eldest brother had taken admission in the Bachelor of Science degree after completing his school education while continuing with his work on the field. Now every member of the family pinned their hopes on him, waiting for him to get a job. That would improve the financial condition of the family drastically.

Back in those days, only those with small holdings were left in the village. The yields from their fields barely helped to sustain their families, leave aside savings and growth. These people did not have the resources to send their children to big schools or colleges in far off cities.

Quite naturally then, most parents with the usual outlook expect their children to contribute to the household financially. And because the children are also aware of their parent's expectations and conditions in the house, they are mentally prepared to take up a job soon after schooling.

In such a situation, they have just two options with respect to employment – firstly, joining the Army as a soldier, and secondly, joining the police force as a constable. And because these are the only options they know of, the child also starts preparing accordingly. While some get selected in the first attempt, others have to try multiple times before they get lucky.

Unfortunately, there is no dearth of those in our society who point fingers at others. Especially at those who cannot get selected in the very first attempt. Someone who gets selected in the first go is stamped as talented. His parents are praised for his good upbringing.

To my mind, this is quite unfair because all parents bring up their children to the best of their ability. After all, no one wants his or her child to be lacking in good qualities. But who can stop a person who has a sharp tongue and loves criticizing! Consequently, life becomes challenging for those whose children don't make it even after a number of attempts.

The moment he finished schooling, Bhaiya had also become eligible for joining the Army. He would make it a point of going to all such places where recruitment tests were being held for the Army or the Police. He had tried many times, but success had eluded him. All of us were waiting for him to be selected.

Finally, in 1995, he was selected for a technical post. When his name appeared in the final merit list, all of us were beside ourselves with happiness. Everyone was happy, except my mother. After all, Bhaiya helped my mother the most in farming. Maa was happy at his selection, but she was also worried. Who would share her load in the field? She was scared that we would slide back to the same situation that we had found ourselves in almost eight years back. This was because Papa had still not recovered from his illness.

But all that aside, I was thrilled that Bhaiya had got a job. Now he would bring clothes and sweets for us when he came home. I had seen a few people from the neighbourhood do that and was rather hopeful that we would see the same days soon.

I told my mother, 'Now stop worrying about the work in the fields. I promise that I will look after all the work. I will show you that I can work equally hard and the harvest will be the same. Maybe even better.'

When my brother heard what I had said, he was very happy. Earlier, he had explained all the intricacies of farming and how to get the best out of land to me while I had worked with him. He was hoping that the balance at home would not be disrupted with his departure.

Finally, when it was time for him to go on his training, he took ten days and explained each and every possible detail he could think of. Very lovingly, he explained how to work without feeling the pressure, how to conduct myself in the society and several such things.

I listened to him carefully and promised that I would never let the family down and never compromise with its honour.

My mother was sad for quite some time after Bhaiya left. With great difficulty, I managed to bring her back to the normal state and started my work, to fulfill my promise. When the grain was harvested that season, the yield of wheat was greater than when my brother used to work.

I had made a promise and now everyone could see that it was being fulfilled. There were tears of joy in my eyes. I realized at that moment that it takes more than just words to fulfill a promise. It takes hard work, sincerity, honesty and most importantly, faith in god.

I loved my field, cattle and harvest. I loved every situation that I went through and tackled all of them in a responsible manner. And for every stepping stone, I offered my thanks to god. This is what my father had always taught me – 'When we do some work honestly and sincerely, god is pleased and grants us a fourfold return for our hard work.'

It was due to Papa's lessons and Bhaiya's great love that I was able to shoulder the entire responsibility of the household and do it resolutely.

> *The other name of life is pain. We need to endure pain at every step if we wish to be the best version of ourselves.*

5

Family as an Inspiration

Words of encouragement from Papa and Bhaiya changed my life completely. It is said that if younger children go by the example set by their elder sibling and parents, nobody can stop them from attaining success in life. Their words, coloured by their experience, help in improving the quality of our present life. Their teachings also lay down a strong foundation for future prospects as well.

That's one thing in contrast that I notice nowadays. I feel, these days, the youth focuses only on the present. And if you try to reason with them, they will have arguments to counter every point.

Honestly, they are right in some matters. After all, who knows what will happen in the future. But it is equally true that a strong foundation laid in the present helps to pave the way for a stronger and more attractive future. If the foundation is weak, the building might look attractive, but it won't be strong and lasting.

Just think for yourself, will a building with a weak foundation be able to endure the forces of nature? No! It will topple over like a house of cards if it has to face torrential rains or strong storms. It would be like a pile of sand which cannot withstand even a light shower or a strong breeze. I feel one should make constant efforts to strengthen the foundation of the present with hard work and sincerity.

Let me give you an example as a farmer. Not many of you might know, but a farmer, while sowing the seed, has to do so at a certain depth in the soil. That is to make sure that the seed does not flow away on watering the field. In the same way, children should sow the seed of knowledge in their mind at a certain depth so that it is retained forever. This is a sure shot way to success. As a child, Bhaiya and Papa inspired me in this way – sowing knowledge at the right depth, nurturing it in the right way.

Since Papa had served in the Army and Bhaiya was also a part of it, they inspired me to join the Army and serve my country. In 1996, Bhaiya had come home after completing his training. When all of us were sitting together and the matter of my joining the Army came up, I said jokingly, 'I don't want to enlist now. I have not even reached the eligible age. I have just taken admission in class twelve. So I will think about it after finishing school.'

Much after I had said this to him, I gave the issue some thought at night, while going to bed. There was a conflict in my mind. I think confusion always gives clarity to one's thinking. I thought Bhaiya was only telling me how I could fulfill my dream.

After all, I had always wanted to see myself in the Army uniform, fighting for my country.

To be honest, night time was my introspection time. Maybe because Papa would tell stories about the 1965 and 1971 wars to his friends while puffing away at his hookah. Even as a child, I would sit near him, listening to his stories very carefully. Perhaps all those accounts of bravery shown by soldiers had made a deep impression on my subconscious mind. Often, I had these dreams because of them, but I lived those dreams with all my heart and soul.

The words of encouragement from Papa and Bhaiya gave wings to my dreams. I felt that nobody could now stop me from fulfilling them. As the first step towards this, I started collecting information on how to go about it – when the recruitment would take place and what papers I would need to be able to take part in it. I got to know from the recruitment office that the tests would be in October, so I started preparing for it as best as I could.

Neither was I very good at studies, nor did I have a strong physique, but I was confident that I would get selected in the very first attempt. This was primarily because I had great confidence in myself.

My mother had told me, 'It is self-confidence which rewards us with success. If you have faith in yourself, you will get selected in the first go.'

These loving words gave me a lot of courage. I wanted to be fully prepared and put in my best efforts for the same.

On the flip side, I think Papa and Bhaiya had some doubt about my resolve. I don't know if that was because Bhaiya had to try really hard for it, or because they thought I was young and needed to put in more efforts. My mother's faith got me through the selection process for physical endurance in the very first go on 10 October 1996. I was ecstatic.

The physical exam was conducted through long distance running and I aced it. Then I cleared the written test and medical examination, which completed my selection process into the Indian Army.

I had to travel to Meerut thrice for this entire process to be completed. Maa would give me hundred rupees when I would leave home with the parting words, 'Do well, and don't spend all this money. Try to save some of it.'

We had seen such tough days at home that we were always mostly conservative in our approach. And Meerut was not very close by as well. The bus ticket to Meerut from my village cost twenty-five rupees. Since students got discount in local buses, I managed to save some money on the fare. So after paying about fifteen rupees on the bus, I shelled out another ten rupees for rickshaw fare to my sister's house. This way, I managed to save fifty rupees most of the time. Only once, I spent close to ten rupees on some food because I was starving.

In this context, I remember something funny which I had to go through. During the selection process, I had to eat a dozen bananas and drink a lot of water before my weight was checked. This was because my weight was a little less than the mentioned weight. And, this was the only quick fix I could think of on such short notice.

By putting all my efforts in this direction, I finally got selected for the Army on 27 December 1996 and fulfilled my most cherished dream with the blessings of my family.

> *Thoughtful people, who are full of good qualities, are humble. It's the empty vessels that make much noise.*

6

The Unique Village Lifestyle

Do you know that there are close to 6,64,369[2] villages in India? Just imagine the number of people in India who live in villages! Our country is known for its rich cultural heritage. It is equally true that each village has its own customs and traditions. Each region has its own language, way of dressing and eating habits.

Ours is such a vast country that language dialect changes with every step you take. So quite naturally, the villages in my region also have a different set languages and traditions. When people sit together and talk during evenings, keeping all these differences in mind, it is very interesting. This diversity presents a very colourful picture which is sure to fill one with great delight.

2. 2019 Census by Government of India.

I have always felt that I have a more balanced and secular outlook towards life. And if I give a deeper it thought, I will find that it stems from my experiences in my village. It might surprise you to learn that in some villages, people of different castes and religions live together with great warmth and understanding, sharing all their happiness and sorrows. I loved this picture of harmony right from my childhood.

Let me recount a small incident from my childhood that laid the foundation for my flexible and open-minded attitude. I remember that there were only two or three Muslim families in our village. They worked as carpenters and ironsmiths. Whatever wooden or iron things had to be made or replaced in the entire village, they were the ones who did it.

All of a sudden, one day, the ironsmith's son was diagnosed with jaundice. He had to be taken to Delhi. The poor man did not have the money or means to take the child to Delhi. Some people in the village took him in their car and got him admitted to a good hospital. Everyone in the village contributed and the money was sent to Delhi to pay for the medical expenses. Despite that, there was no improvement in the condition of the child.

A few days later we heard about the sad demise of the child. Everyone in the village was stunned. When his body came to the village, everyone took part in the burial. That was honestly the kind of sight we see when a soldier, who has died for his country, is taken on his last journey. I witnessed a scene like this as a five-year-old for the first time in my life. To this day, the sight of this funeral procession is deeply etched in my memory.

I feel proud when I recollect those days. I always remember the selfless love people had for each other and how they helped wholeheartedly in times of adversities and grief. It was like one big family, where the mutual bond was very close. Even today, when I think about it, I feel thrilled. That's what ingrained the love for fellow Indians in me from the very start. When I went into the Army and fought for the nation, I was not doing it for any one religion, caste or person – I was doing it for all my brothers and sisters who make this country what it is.

However, with the rapid change in lifestyle across the whole world, its impact is also seen in the villages. But despite that, even today, people in villages have the same degree of love and respect for each other. They are always ready to help in hours of need. I noticed this every time I went back home on leave.

♋

I remember, as a child, when Maa cooked on the *chulha* in the evening, we would sit around her and have our dinner. There was just one room anyway, so the luxury of a dining table was unimaginable. Papa would also eat with us and in the course of dinner, would tell Maa about our good qualities as well as shortcomings. We would feel encouraged with this and also learn of our weaknesses. When he started talking about my shortcomings, I would feel so embarrassed that at times it was difficult to continue eating.

If you think this is a critical approach, or that he was insulting us or demotivating us, I won't agree. I would say that it requires a sense of balance. He praised us wholeheartedly; he criticized us with all honesty. Maybe that is why we were inspired to grow as a person. And this sort of thing was not limited to just our family; the scene was the same in all houses in the neighbourhood.

To this day, when I go to my village, I prefer to have my meals in this way with my brothers. Of course, the food is not cooked on a chulha anymore, but the spirit of togetherness in the family remains intact.

When I see children making a fuss while eating these days, I remember my childhood days. As against the multiple options we have today and the luxury to afford them, Maa used to give us curd in a big bowl and some chapattis. Vegetables grown in our field were cooked only once a day. In the evening, we would have our rotis with chutney made of tomatoes and onions, some jaggery and milk. Perhaps that taught us to appreciate every small thing we get.

By now, you must have realized that people in villages have a unique lifestyle. I bow to people in my village as well as my country, who live harmoniously in spite of belonging to different religions, castes and creeds. It is this unity, mutual faith, selfless love and harmony that give strength to our country.

The day you stop putting in the efforts is the day you stop growing.

7

Unity in Diversity

Coming from a village background gave me a different and unique picture of togetherness and unity. I noticed that in most villages, people are full of love for each other and always ready to help in the hour of need. They treat everyone as their own, without stopping to think about the differences that might be there. When you meet them, you will realize how sincere and diligent they are. They have full faith in their hard work and god also looks after them, testing them sometimes.

Since India is an agriculture-based community in general, the people in villages depend on their crop for growth and sustenance. They have no other source of earning their livelihood. I have seen the entire crop being destroyed by heavy rains or hailstorms at times. Despite these heavy losses, god sees to it that they get enough to eat and don't have to beg from anyone.

These small incidents go a long way and make the most difference in one's life. Looking at my peers and their families brave all odds with a smile, I learned to face difficult times and situations without accepting defeat. God is sure to help you if you have firm faith in yourself.

♋

Let me tell you my first experience of learning how a team works and what unity can do! To tell you the truth, unity is as deeply embedded in village people as fragrance is integral to a rose. A similar unity can be seen among bees – if someone throws a stone at their hive, all the bees get together and chase him away. In the same way, if an outsider tries to harm anyone in the village, the whole community unites and surrounds him and his family, forming a protective circle.

I remember an incident from childhood. I must be roughly in class six or seven at that time. In those days, a *harijan*[3] family used to live on the eastern side of our village. It was winter and their daughter was supposed to get married in a few days. They had been toiling day and night to accumulate all essentials for the wedding, including clothes, jewellery and gifts.

Some goons attacked their house. When they were going away after looting all that had been bought for the wedding, they fired in the air to show their bravado. They wanted to show that they could rob a house in a village that hadn't seen any theft till now. I feel, this was not bravery in any way, but a mark of cowardice. But in that situation, they were challenging the unity of our village.

---

3. Scheduled Caste

Soon after, they must have realized how wrong they were. As soon as there was the sound of firing, everyone in the village came out with whatever weapons they could get a hand on – lathis (sticks), shovels, knives and even guns. In a trice, they reached the house which had been robbed.

The people in the family told them the direction in which the criminals had gone. In a matter of minutes, people could hear firing again. Though the criminals had revolvers and most of the villagers had only lathis, the latter fought bravely like soldiers who fight for the glory of their country and the national flag. It was a question of their self-respect and honour of the village. No one cared about their life. A fellow had been looted and they had to protect the sanctity of the village. If they didn't retaliate now, this could happen again and they wanted to nip this in the bud.

The conflict continued for quite a few hours. But eventually, the thieves were taken care of and the looted articles were restored to the family.

At that time, I felt proud of the unity among the people of my village. Not just that, this incident inspired even the children in the community to look after the safety of their fellow villagers.

All of us took up the resolve that come what may, we would never let the honour of our village be sullied. This instilled the feeling of unity and togetherness among us. I cultivated this sentiment in my heart and it proved to be very useful to me in the Army. There, your Unit, the people around you, are your family. They celebrate with you in your happy moments and stand by your side when the time is challenging, so the lesson went a long way.

♋

Have you ever wondered what cooperation really means? The word instantly suggests helping someone even without being asked to do so. Help can be extended in any way. It could be by supporting someone who is specially-abled to cross the road or to get into a vehicle. It could involve helping the aged or assisting someone who is not able to lift something heavy in spite of trying a number of times. Helping in any way, big or small, is cooperation. An incident which took place when I was still young is still deeply etched in my memory.

I still tremble when I think about it. At the same time, the help extended by my friends and neighbours sends a chill down my spine.

It was the month of May. Harvesting is usually over by May-June and some stubble is left in the fields. On the western side of our village, there was a field where hay had been stacked. We didn't know how, but a fire broke out there. Now, May and June are hot months, ideal for a fire to spread in an uncontrolled manner. It was afternoon when the fire broke out. As it is, the rays of the sun had dried up all the greenery. It needed just a spark to burn everything to cinders and that is what happened.

Along with the fury of Agni, the fire god, Pawan, the god of wind gave a helping hand and the fire looked as if it would burn up the entire village. The fire spread in the direction of the wind rapidly.

In a short while, our house was caught in the fury of the spreading flames. Everyone in the village was trying their best to control the fire with whatever resources they could lay their hands on. They were organized like an army, fighting a common enemy. But the fire god would not be appeased. It seemed he had decided to burn the whole village down.

I had just come back from a visit to the doctor with my mother when I saw this. I had a high fever. Despite the sedation of the medicine, I opened my eyes when I heard the cries and screams of people and witnessed the terrible scene. Our house had only one concrete room, the others had thatched roofs. When I got up from my cot, I saw that there was smoke all around. There was total chaos. Some people were running to save the cattle, others were cutting their ropes and taking them out.

Maa instructed sharply, "Run towards the temple with your brothers!' When I ran towards the temple on the southern side of the village, I noticed that all our farming implements were being burnt down. However, by that time, twelve fire engines had arrived. With the help of the villagers and the fire engines, the fire was finally put out.

By the time the situation could be brought under control, it was evening. Our entire locality had been reduced to ashes. Nothing remained – fodder for the cattle, grain, cots and clothes. Everything had been burnt to ashes by the fire. In the evening, some could be seen looking for their children, others for their cattle. It was a pitiful sight.

It was past ten at night. We kept on staring at our charred belongings. Maa just wouldn't stop crying; she was in a bad state. People from the nearby localities were crowding around, in all the houses. The whole day had been spent in fighting the fire and now we were beside ourselves with hunger. Around eleven at night, some food came, cooked by our neighbours and we had it. But there was no place to sleep, no cots, nothing to cover ourselves with. Anyway, we slept on the floor and somehow the night passed. In the morning, people in the village gave us some clothes.

The whole of the next day was spent in removing the ashes from our belongings and slowly, with the help of our village people, we tried to get back to normal life. I remember, Papa had made a firm resolution that day. From then on, we would never build a house with a thatched roof. For the time being, we put up a tin roof and began saving for the future. As time passed, we built a brick house.

But imagine such a calamity befalling someone who has no financial support of insurance. In such cases, safety and starting afresh are not possible without the help of fellow people in the society.

When our house was burnt down, our family needed help. People in the village came forward to extend it wholeheartedly. I understood how the smallest gesture fills the recipient with confidence and gives them the courage to put in more efforts.

It is this episode that made me imbibe the quality of always extending a helping hand to others in need. Even a small gesture can change someone's life.

Love is the source of all your energy. The more you tap into your inner reserves of love, the greater you get love from the others.

8

The Saga of my Stubbornness

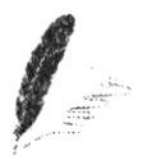

You must have experienced that a child is influenced by the company he keeps early in life. This is why parents always insist on the right kind of friends for their children. Many teachers have talked about it and ancient texts have also referred to it. When I look back, I realize that the company I kept influenced me a lot. I became dogged, but in a positive way, something which always inspired me to move ahead in life.

Let me tell you a few instances which shaped me in a way that paved the foundation for my never give up attitude.

In the olden days, there used to be fairs in the village during Dussehra and Diwali. This brought a pleasant change in our lives. The most attractive feature was Ramlila. For the benefit of those who are not familiar with the legend, Dussehra celebrates the victory of Rama over Ravana and Diwali is a festival that marks the arrival of Rama in Ayodhya after his victory. During the Navratri, the nine-day festival that precedes Dussehra, the story of Rama and Ravana is presented as a play which culminates in the grand finale when Ravana is killed by Rama.

These days, the significance of this tradition has dwindled considerably, but at that time, very well known actors would come to take part in the Ramlila. They would perform so brilliantly that they left a profound impression on the audience.

There used to be a Ramlila performance staged near our house every year and all of us would go there, right from our childhood. After the performance was over, Maa would return home and the children would linger for a while with their friends.

I must have been in class five. Some boys of the village, who had come to watch Ramlila, sat together after the performance and had tobacco. I would also sit with them. Since it had started getting cold, I would soon feel sleepy. I noticed that all the boys had tobacco and did not feel drowsy.

One day, they offered me some tobacco as well. I did not know what it was and had it innocently. But soon after, I got addicted to it and started having it every day. Eventually, I picked up the habit of smoking *bidis* too.

By the time I was in sixth standard, I had begun drinking with those friends. It was the festival of Holi. I got so drunk that I did not know where I was. For a while, I lay in a stupor at my neighbour's house and later in the afternoon, members of my family picked me up from there and brought me home.

I was told later that Maa and Papa gave me buttermilk. They poured cold water on my head, gave me mango pickle and generally resorted to all the home remedies that are usually done in such crises. I did not realize when it was morning.

When I woke up, I was asked questions about my drinking. I said that I had drunk half a bottle of liquor and then had water from the nearby tap. Maa asked where I had got the liquor from. I told her that all my friends had contributed twenty rupees each, and with that they had bought the liquor bottle. Papa asked their names. Then he brought them to our house, and along with Bhaiya, gave them a sound thrashing. After that, I stopped sitting with those boys and tried to occupy myself in other ways. I drank *bhang* only once a year on the day of Holi as was customary in the village. When everyone in my family saw that I did not have any such habits anymore that needed to be monitored, they stopped taking any notice of it.

My father used to drink once in a while, especially on days when it was freezing. He was an ex-serviceman and got liquor bottles for himself from the Army canteen. At night, when he sat with his friends or by himself, he would tell me to prepare two pegs for him. I would quietly drink some from the glass and pour in water to make the portion appear the same.

I had even noticed that Papa used to count the pegs he was having and total up the amount left in the bottle. So naturally, when I poured in extra water to cover up, he was not able to make out what had happened.

Then, something happened after a few months. It was summer and I was sleeping on the terrace. My *tauji's*[4] son had got married two or three days back. Papa had gone to visit a relative's place and Maa and my brothers were at home. Bhaiya

4. Father's elder brother

and Maa would get up early by habit, to start the day's work. I would get up and go down a little later. That was because I had to smoke a bidi at that time.

That particular day, when I was smoking, my elder brother came up. When I heard him coming up the stairs, I quickly put out the bidi, but there was no way of hiding the smoke.

My brother could easily make out that someone had smoked there. He asked me angrily, 'Were you smoking?'

I denied it straight away, but he just wouldn't listen to me. When he smelled my mouth, he could make out the truth. He looked under the bed sheet and found the packet of bidis. He broke the packet and gave me a sound slap. Then he went back downstairs and told Maa; she was also furious. I was very young then. I was not able to make out why so much fuss was being made about such a trivial thing. I could not understand why everyone was holding me guilty.

In a fit of anger, I lay on the cot the whole day. Maa came to call me to have food twice, once she even brought food for me, but I refused. I told her that I would eat only when she would let me smoke.

Now I realize that it was a very childish way to behave, but at that time, I did not think so. Children often don't realize the gravity of what they have done; they are not mature enough to do so.

Anyway, the whole day passed and then, the whole night. I stuck to my bed and refused to get up. My mother told the neighbours, that I was not having my food. I was just lying on my cot, sulking. The next morning, some neighbours came to placate me and make me have my food. I refused, giving everyone the same answer that I would eat only when allowed to smoke.

Well, they were all grown up people and weren't going to let me smoke. So I also refused to have food. Almost four days passed in this way. Papa returned home on the fifth day, in the evening. He heard about my antics from my mother and brother in detail. Without the slightest trace of showing any annoyance, he asked me, 'What do you want?'

Pointing towards my brother, I said in an innocent manner, 'He has broken my bundle of bidis. I want a bidi.'

As soon as he heard this, my father lost all control and started beating me with a stick. My tauji's elder son and my brother also followed suit. I was beaten like a thief who had been caught red-handed. I thought I would die if this continued. There was only one way to get away from this. I decided to run away.

Mustering all my strength, I pushed them away and ran downstairs. I kept on running till I reached the Gang *nahar* (canal), about two kilometers away. Both my brothers were running after me, shouting. Harvesting was going on in the field and my brothers kept on shouting for the farmers to catch me, '*Pakdo, pakdo*!'

I wonder how I had so much energy even after remaining hungry and thirsty for five days. I looked back and saw that several people were running after me. Everyone thought I would jump into the canal. I did not know how to swim so there was no question of jumping into the canal. I kept running along the side of the canal with everyone chasing me. Suddenly, I had such a severe stomach ache that it became impossible for me to walk any further, leave aside running.

There was a mango orchard on the side of the canal. I lay there before being caught eventually. My brothers brought me home, beating me on the way. I came home, lay down on the cot, but still refused to eat.

After a couple of days, my father's friend, who was in the U.P. Police, came to our house. When he heard about this from my father, he took me to his house and pleaded with me to have food. I said, 'There is food in my house too. What I want first is a bidi.'

Seven days had passed and I was in very bad shape. He realized the gravity of the matter and gave me a bidi. 'Here, you can have it!'

I smoked the bidi quietly and came back home. I did not have any food in his house, just smoked the bidi and came back. In hindsight, I realize that it was just a mark of my stubbornness.

When night came, I got time to introspect and ponder over the last few days. Next morning, I got up at five, heaped all the dung on the bullock cart and went towards the fields. No one said anything. They were not talking to me. I felt I had been shamed. I had made a laughing stock of myself in front of everyone. The only way in which I could make up for it was by hard work. On that day, I made three trips to the field with the cart full of dung.

Papa told Maa, 'He has been working hard since morning, give him some food.'

So Maa came with food and asked me to have something. I also said loftily, 'Yes, I will have food. After all, I have been working so hard.' Without taking help from anyone, I had taken fifteen cartloads of dung to the field.

After that day, I did smoke a bidi some time on the sly, but worked harder than before. I noticed that people who had been critical of me earlier, now praised me. That's when I realized that work is something which has the power to transform the attitude and feelings of people. And it also taught me that if I channelize my stubbornness for a good cause, I will achieve wonders.

I thought back on this episode when I was in Kargil, and reminded myself that I had to stubbornly defend my country, come what may!

> *A person obsessed with his ego can neither see his own shortcomings, nor the goodness of others.*

9

Building Inner Strength

My stubborn nature was popular far and wide by now. So Maa tried to tell me how I could use it in a better way. She taught me that sometimes, stubbornness also increases forbearance in children. It pushes them to work relentlessly in the most adverse conditions, thus making the impossible achievable. Perhaps it is this stubbornness that has helped me to tread the path I have chosen with a firm mind.

I was very obstinate right from my childhood, not content till I had attained something I had set my mind on. I will now tell you another story related to my obstinacy.

One day, Bhaiya hit me for some reason and I went out of the house seething in anger. I spent the whole day in the sugarcane field. Everyone was looking for me as no one had seen me for hours. In the evening, they came to know that I was in the field as someone from the village had seen me there. Papa and Bhaiya came to look for me. I saw them approaching from my position on the tree on which I had perched. To avoid being seen, I hid in the sugarcane field.

They called out to me a number of times, but I kept quiet. When they were about to leave the place, I felt I should let them know that I was there. I climbed a tree and saw them going away. I got down from the tree and looked around me. There were some mango trees nearby. I picked up a stick and hit a mango tree. They could make out from the sound that someone was around, but they couldn't see a thing.

It had become dark and there could be wild animals around. It was common for some wild animals to come strolling into the fields at night. That is why I had planned to spend the night on the tree.

As soon as they heard the sound of the stick, Bhaiya ran towards the sound to catch me. Again, I hid myself behind the tall sugarcane. It was not possible for them to look for me there as it was a very large field. They called out to me again, but I did not answer. Now they knew for sure that I was there.

Bhaiya called out for me loudly, and Papa did the same – sometimes in a loving voice, sometimes using abusive language. But irrespective of that, there was no response from me.

It was past ten on a chilly winter night. My brother didn't want to stay there any longer and decided to head back home. Papa told him, 'Go and get me some warm clothes and food here.'

Bhaiya protested, but Papa insisted that he would spend the night at the field. After Bhaiya left in a huff, I came out of the field.

I knew well that Papa could not run because of his poor health and told him to go home. He told me to come home with him and I said, 'Bhaiya has hit me without any reason. I won't go back till am assured that he will be punished.'

On hearing this, he said, 'That's it? Come home! I will set him straight.'

I was happy to hear that and believed him. I presumed that he would hit my brother once we got home. But quite obviously, that did not happen. Once we reached home, his attitude changed completely. He told my brother to hit me. I stood there, getting beaten. I did not retaliate because I realised that my brother had not hit me for fun; I had been at fault and should have owned up.

Papa was strict when it came to respecting our elders and he had explained this to me several times. When he realized that I had got my lesson, he told me to go and eat something.

Would a child feel like having food after being beaten up in such a way? So naturally, I didn't, and went to bed hungry.

In the morning, I realized that I had made a mistake so I got back to doing my work. I knew that helping everyone at home with their work and making their burden lighter was a better way of apologizing than by saying it in words. After every such incident, something inside me pushed me to work harder and more earnestly, without feeling tired.

Maybe these are the small incidents in life which make a person stronger and increase their tolerance and forbearance.

> *If you want to love, love your family, yourself and your nation. A friend or lover might betray you, but your family and nation will not.*

10

The Trust Factor

I have been amazed to notice how on one hand, the society honours us and gives us the chance to rise in life. But on the other hand, there are people in the same society who take advantage of helpless and weak people. They exploit them fully for their own benefits and try to take away whatever little they have. I learnt it early in life that it is imperative to safeguard oneself from such people, and for that, one must know who they are!

Papa and Bhaiya often told me ways in which we could judge the character of a person and then, plan a way forward. Imagine how handy that could come in the Army, where I was constantly in unknown territories. I think learning this lesson early on in life helped a great deal in my Army tenure.

This incident happened when we were still living in a hut with a thatched roof, supported by bamboo poles. That pole broke and needed to be replaced. Since my brother and I were very young, my mother gave money to a neighbour and asked them to buy whatever was needed for the repair work. They got the material for five hundred rupees, but told us that it had cost eight hundred.

On another occasion, while we were irrigating the field, the engine of the pump broke down. The person who was sent to get it repaired paid a thousand rupees, but told us that it had cost one thousand five hundred. We knew how each penny was earned through our endless hard work. Given the circumstances, every single rupee was worth a fortune.

Consider that a lot of money was being spent on Papa's medical treatment, so we were basically always short of cash at home. After these experiences, we realized that there were people who were determined to rob us of the little money we had. They felt absolutely no pity for us, despite knowing the circumstances we were in. But back then, we could not do anything in spite of knowing the truth. Whatever we could do on our own, we did, but sometimes we had to ask others for help.

We came to know the truth when we started taking over most of the work ourselves. There was pain of being cheated on, but there was immense satisfaction that we were self-dependent now.

I feel it is very essential to be independent. And those who try to benefit from the helplessness of others never prosper in life.

While I pray to god for peace and prosperity in the society and the whole country, I have noticed that such greedy people cannot attain it. Today, they have come down to the lower strata of society while we have worked our way to the hearts of people. In the end, that's all that matters.

Honestly speaking, whether one talks of financial independence, or having one's own house, fields, business or job, the country will succeed only when the children in the family become self-reliant and sincere.

Speaking from my own experience as a child, I understand well that kids do not understand the importance of time. They think in their naiveté that a lot of time is left for them to achieve something big in life. But then, those who want to achieve great heights work hard towards it.

Anyway, how long can one go in life by being dependent on their parents? They will not be there forever. At some point in life, one will have to be on their own. Those who don't learn this early in life will have to face insurmountable problems when they are forced to be independent.

I have seen youngsters who consider their parents like a shady tree – always giving them comfort while themselves choosing to face the harsh realities of life. Such people are unstoppable. With a strong determination, they move forward, sharing their family's burden when they can. Thus, they are able to withstand all problems in life from the very beginning.

> *The ticking of the clock is a marker for progress and change. With every second that passes, we grow a little.*

PART – II

FROM A CIVILIAN TO A SOLDIER

11

Travelling to the Regiment

When I look back, I feel that the childhood days seemed so difficult to bear while I went through them. Now I feel that those were the most carefree days, which won't ever come back. I learnt a lot in my childhood and the experience came in handy when I joined the Army.

All my friends and members of the family knew how eager I was to join the Indian Army. It had been my dream right from the start. So when I was selected and had to report for the training, everyone was overwhelmed. The story of my joining the Army is also a memorable one.

My tauji and his son, who studied with me, accompanied me to the recruitment office on 27 December 1996. We reached there in the afternoon. First, all our documents were checked and verified, a process known as documentation. There were many people there.

When all the formalities were completed, Col. R.K. Singh, overseeing the process of documentation and recruitment, addressed all of us. He made it clear to us that we would have to show courage in the coming days. We were told that we would have to take the evening train to Delhi for the forthcoming training. We were made to sit in an Army vehicle at about 4.30 p.m. Members of the family accompanying the recruits were told that from now on, the Army was in charge of all of us and they could go back home.

My tauji and my cousin stood outside and watched all this. While the vehicle was going out of the gate, I told them, 'You can go home, we'll meet soon.'

But they refused. Instead, they went to the railway station on their own and met me at the platform.

When it was time for the train to leave, my cousin cried a lot. We had studied together, played together and done quite a few notorious things together. He was less a cousin, more a dear friend.

I told him calmly, 'Don't cry, bhai. Look after Maa. And if there is a problem, try to solve it patiently. My younger brother is still very young, so you will have to now watch over him as well.'

I had a feeling that he was crying so much because he was the only one left among the slightly older children. Anyway, I sent him off after explaining things to him as best as I could. He was inconsolable, but there was little that we could do about it.

By that time, our train had also arrived and we started boarding it along with our luggage. There were twenty-one of us and we had to go to The Grenadiers Regimental Centre in Jabalpur.

So I embarked on the journey of my Army life along with these twenty other boys. When we loaded all the luggage on to the train and took our seats, we introduced ourselves to each other. By the time we reached, we were fairly acquainted with each other. Gradually, we had become friends.

Our first destination was Delhi. From there, we were to take a train to Jabalpur – where the Regimental Centre is situated. We sat waiting for the train at New Delhi station, but got to know that our train was from Nizamuddin station – which is on the other end of town. We quickly grabbed our bags and caught a local train to Nizamuddin station. It was past ten at night.

When we asked at the enquiry desk, we found out that the train was at 2.30 the next afternoon. It was the first night that we spent at the railway station and it was very cold. We had to gulp down a lot of tea to stay warm. There was so much commotion at the station that before we realized, it was morning. Half the day passed just by watching the people around us. When the public announcement said that the train for Jabalpur had come to its platform, we got ready to board it.

We grabbed our bags and boarded the unreserved compartment. The journey from Delhi to Jabalpur was spent in a jovial mood, laughing and singing. Finally, we reached Jabalpur the next morning. The train journey was over, but for me, this was the beginning of another journey – a new life with the Indian Army.

When we came out of the station, we saw an Army bus waiting for us. A Havaldar saw us and said, 'Those going to the Grenadiers, get into this bus!'

We took our luggage and got into the bus. The Havaldar then asked, 'Have you come from Meerut?'

We answered in unison, 'Yes sir.'

When we had started from Meerut, a commander had been nominated for us. He had all the papers related to our recruitment. Most of the time, he did the talking and asking questions because we could not move around much with the entire luggage. The Havaldar talked to the commander for quite some time and when both of them were satisfied, the bus started towards the Grenadiers Regimental Centre.

Since it was close by, just about three or four kilometers from the railway station, we reached there in no time. Upon entering the gates of the Centre, our bus stopped near the Adjutant's office. We got down with our luggage and were asked to stand in a queue. We did as we were told and a Subedar arrived along with a Havaldar, who had RP written on the band on his arm. Later, we came to know that he was a Regimental Police Company Havaldar Major and the other one was the Subedar Adjutant of the Centre.

He said at once, 'Oh, you are from Meerut? You must be having 312 or 325 bore locally made rifles with you!' Perhaps, he wanted to make the atmosphere lighter and referred to our district's notorious image of making illegal weapons.

We said in a chorus, 'No sir.'

He smiled on noticing that we knew he had been joking. I mustered some courage and said, 'Sir, the district of Meerut is also famous for the brave men it has produced, who are ready to put their lives at stake for their country.'

After this, our luggage was checked. All of us picked up our bags and stood in a line. We were sent with the Havaldar to go and have our breakfast.

Post breakfast, we waited for our turn for verification of documents. By the time the documents were checked, it was already noon. As soon as all the formalities were completed, we were sent to different training companies.

Out of the 21 boys who had been recruited and sent for training, 7 had been sent to 2TC, that is Training Centre no 2. I was one of them.

The stillness of the lake is disturbed when we throw in a pebble. Similarly, when we give our mind a purpose, our mind works towards achieving it.

12

My First Day at the Regimental Centre

Ever since I had joined the Army, I had been rather excited about the Grenadiers Regimental Centre. It was the auspicious day of 29 December 1996 when we stepped into the Centre. The journey was rather long. I am not talking about the actual journey by train, but my personal one, which included my long-term dream of being a part of the Indian Army.

When we reached the Centre, the first thing I saw was Company Quartermaster Havaldar Abdul Hamid's jeep. He had been in 4 Grenadiers and had been awarded the Param Vir Chakra posthumously. When I saw the jeep, I wondered whether anyone would ever take my name so proudly. Would I ever fulfill the dream of doing something great for my country?

As I was walking towards my Company with these thoughts flitting in my mind, I noticed the Major Hoshiar Singh PVC Parade Ground. I was finally seeing the ground I had read about and heard of from elders in the village. It was a wonderful feeling to have. With such inspirational sights all around me, I started my training.

The seven of us in 2TC were assigned the South Platoon. Since the documents had already been checked, we were sent to our respective platoon immediately. We had lunch there and went off to sleep, tired after the long journey.

At about 3 p.m., we were served tea. We were instructed to get ready and wait in front of the adjacent shop.

'Go, everyone will have a haircut now!' the Ustad said. I knew that we would have to go through this, but had not realized it would be so early. The Ustad smiled and said, 'Style your hair as much as you want. You will not get the chance again, at least not in your career in the Army.'

What he said was absolutely correct. Twenty-five years have passed since that day, but our hair has never grown long enough to style it differently. All of us sat in a row outside the shop. One by one, the barber gave all of us a crew cut. We laughed at each other's hair, but soon we realized that we looked alike and came back to the centre.

This was our first taste of the discipline in the Army. By the evening, everyone had their hair cut. Then we were given the khaki uniform. Among the other things that had been given were – two blades, two blankets, one to spread on the cot and the other to cover oneself, a mosquito net, a rug and a white mug for tea. As per the strict discipline, we had been instructed about how to fold the mosquito net in the morning after using it at night.

After all this was over, we went to the dining room to have our dinner. I had a big bowl which my mother had given me. I put ghee in it from my bag and took it along to have with food. Dal, cooked vegetables and roti were served that night. There was lively chatter over the meal as everyone was in good spirits.

As soon as we reached our barrack after dinner, we heard a whistle being blown. This meant that we all had to assemble in one place. We had been instructed about it earlier during the welcome address. So all of us stood on the spot where we had been told to get together. The Senior Junior Commissioned Officer (JCO) and Company Havaldar Major instructed us to proceed to the dining room.

The dining hall was big, but the number of trainees was also very large. All of us were stuffed into the room and all the doors and windows were closed. Since this happened all of a sudden, we could not really understand what was going on. All the ustads of the company were also inside.

Then there was another announcement, 'All ustads should go and get sticks.'

Immediately, all the ustads went and got their sticks. In that moment, I honestly got scared for a bit. All this was too much and beyond our comprehension.

Then we were told, 'Lie down in the hall and take rounds of it, rolling.' I was surprised to hear this, but there was no time to think. Then came a roaring command, 'All of you will pick up the pieces of *rotis* on the ground with your mouth.' The Ustad sounded so angry that in our haste, we almost lay down on each other. The ustads started hitting us with their sticks if we stopped in between or did not do as guided.

I realized that it was a punishment meted out for some seniors' fault. It was given to the whole group as per a custom in the Army. Even if one person is at fault, the entire group is punished. Later we came to know that some of the senior boys who were about to finish their training, had thrown pieces of roti on the floor, which came under the feet of others. Everyone was being punished for that.

When the senior JCO noticed the way food was being disrespected, he made up his mind to teach everyone a lesson. At that time, we found the punishment too harsh, but later, when we came to know the reason behind it, I thought it had been absolutely just. I don't know the name of that particular JCO, but I salute him wholeheartedly for the way he taught us a valuable lesson.

A person leaves his home and wanders here and there, slogging throughout his life, just for food. But when he finds it, he disrespects it. He even finds fault with food, calling it overcooked or undercooked and throws away bits and pieces of it. How shameful!

Our seniors had done that by throwing pieces of roti. So we all were made to roll around for an hour, till all the pieces of the chapattis had been eaten up. After that, we were told to stand up. Though it was winter, all of us were soaked in sweat.

Later, the senior JCO asked, 'Are the boys who have joined today also present here?'

That question pierced through my heart, making me think why he hadn't asked this question before starting off the punishment. But today, I think it is good that he remembered it later. The very first day, we were taught to respect food, otherwise we might have behaved like our seniors someday. Who knows!

From that day onwards, I have neither disrespected food myself, nor let anyone do it in my presence. I think it is a relationship of mutual respect – if we respect what we eat, it gives us the energy to stand up to challenges each day.

Gratitude is the most underrated emotion. The more we show gratefulness for what we are blessed with, the more we open up to receiving more from the universe.

13

Time and Tide Wait for None

The experiences on the first day of my training are still firmly imprinted in my mind – a blend of sweet and tangy memories. Even today I remember how I wanted my first day to be memorable. I wanted to retained it in my mind and heart all my life. Maybe that is why I am able to describe everything clearly, along with all the details.

I remember my first day like the back of my hand. We got up at 4 a.m. Since washrooms had to be shared, there was some chaos. Some boys were shaving with a mirror on their trunks. Everyone was busy, happily talking to each other. By the time we were ready, it was past 5.30. I realized that we had to take arms from the armoury as well because in the second parade, we would be told about them. The first parade was Physical Training (PT).

By the time we reached the armoury, it was quite late. The Havaldar on duty had started giving out punishments. I knew that we were late and by the time all of us reached the ground, everyone had already assembled there. The seniors had to send the report and all of us had reached late. We were punished so severely by the PT instructor that it cannot be put into words.

I was asked to do frontal rolls, and there was no count given. It seemed that my world was turning upside down. My head was spinning too. On top of that, the physical instructor kept on hitting us with a rope. But I noticed that everyone, despite feeling giddy and sick, was putting up with the punishment. This went on for about forty minutes. I could have fainted if this went on for another minute. I was wondering when this torture would end. It seemed as if we were being tortured by Pakistani soldiers who had taken us prisoners.

As the physical instructor hit us, he said, 'Do you think you are guests here? Relaxing and shaving at leisure!'

We kept on promising him that we would never be late, never even shave with the cream. That was how forty minutes passed and the bell rang for the second parade.

When we were released for the second parade, I was feeling so sick that I thought I would faint and fall any minute. As I wondered if the others were feeling the same way, I heard the instructor saying, 'Sit down for a while.'

When our heads seemed to have stabilized, we got up, took our weapons and reached the training area. The Platoon Havaldar, who was still angry with us for getting up late in the morning, met us. His face was still red with anger and he said in a loud voice, 'Have your breakfast quickly and come back!'

I realized that from now on, we would have to do everything faster. Our breakfast had already been served in the training area. We took off our PT uniform and changed our dress. Then, we had two puris, drank tea and got ready with our weapons for our training.

It is important to point out here that the Platoon Havaldar is like a mother in the training centre. A mother might be furious with her child, but holds him if he is not feeling well. That day when he saw us, he asked with a smile, 'Are you all right?'

We were very scared that he would scold us once again, but felt relieved when we saw his smile.

Then he explained the finer nuances of the training to us, along with some unsaid rules. His behaviour and the way he spoke reminded me of my parents and the way they used to share things with me.

'Now you are no longer civilians. You are about to become soldiers. A soldier is always conscious of the time at his disposal. Don't waste time on dressing up. Get up early, get ready, clean up your area and report for training.'

As he said it, I wondered how early I would have to get up every day. He seemed to have read my thoughts and said, 'Just thirty minutes. If you get up thirty minutes earlier, you would be able to finish all your work and you will reach everywhere on time.'

Then he looked straight into my eyes and said, 'Then no one will say anything to you.'

From that day, till the end of the training, I shaved without applying shaving cream. I started getting up at 3.30 a.m. You must be thinking that it would still be the dead of the night. It was! But it seemed tough only for a week. Slowly, I got used to it and woke up by myself at that hour almost every day. The training continued for nine months and I was never late again after the first day. On most days, I would get ready and reach before the scheduled time.

On the first day of the training, we learnt the value of time. Today I understand the full significance of that lesson. Time is a very valuable resource. The time lost today never comes back tomorrow.

> *The breath you draw today, the life you live today, will not be there tomorrow. That is why one should know the importance of time and utilize it properly.*

14

The Journey from a Civilian to a soldier

The instructors at the Grenadiers Regimental Centre were very impressive. I can vouch for the fact that the instructor in Training Company 2 was not only a teacher, but like a father figure. By now, the routine for the training was familiar to all of us. We got up every morning, cleaned our personal area, filled up drinking water in the pitcher and got ready in a disciplined manner.

The training taught us to look after our physical development. At the same time, we learnt how to control our emotions and work in coordination with others. I felt very proud to know that the principle of "one for all and all for one" is considered very important in the Army. As I have said before, all were punished for the fault of one and we looked after each other as best as we could.

The first few lessons we learnt during training was cooperation, togetherness, firm resolution and patience. Not only this, it was very important to work in coordination with one another.

I learnt not to go alone anywhere, and collaborate with other members of my team as much as possible. It was ingrained in us that we should be with at least one team member at all times. The Army practices a 'buddy' system where each soldier is given a companion, and they are to stick together at all times. Looking back, I realize that togetherness breeds so much love and companionship that life becomes impossible without your buddy. This buddy becomes like a member of your family.

With such a close relationship, it becomes inevitable to share everything related to your home and family with your buddy. Whether it is a problem related to the family or a piece of news that makes you happy, everything is discussed. This generates mutual trust and love and one is ready to stake everything for one's buddy. You may not understand this fellow feeling, but for a soldier, it is a matter of life and death. A soldier moves on fearlessly because he knows that his buddy is always by his side.

My training continued for nine months. Being addressed as a regimental comrade left an indelible impression on my mind. Taking the name of the regiment constantly makes the impression still deeper. It becomes so deeply embedded in one's mind that even when one is on his deathbed, if the name of the company, regiment or a comrade is spoken out aloud, one sits up.

These are the feelings that slowly transform a civilian into a soldier. A civilian can help his close friends or family members with money, but only in rare cases would he be ready to give his life for them. But a soldier can risk his life without hesitation for his comrade.

These feelings were generated in us through our rigorous training and the environment that we were a part of. As such feelings were formed, they impacted my thinking, behaviour, ideology and the way of working.

If you start thinking, you will realize that it is a person's style of working and behaviour that takes him forward. A soldier always functions in a selfless manner and his behaviour is different from those who work with other organizations.

An Indian soldier is always deeply conscious of the heritage of his country. The fact that a civilian thinks only of himself and his family, cannot be refuted. But a soldier thinks first of his country, then his fellow soldiers and in the end of himself and his family. If a civilian thinks this way, he does not remain a civilian. This feeling had come into my heart now and I realized that I was now a complete soldier – with the right kind of behaviour, ideology and work ethics.

A soldier will think of the country and its people much before he thinks of himself. That completed my transformation from a civilian to a soldier.

15

Knowledge is Power

As the training progressed on a brisk scale, I was learning a lot of new things. There were different kinds of trainings and I learnt something new from each. Sometimes I felt a little apprehensive, but my fears were soon put to rest. We were gaining a lot of self confidence and developing our own opinion on matters related to ourselves.

All organizations teach their employees a sense of judgment in keeping with their work culture and environment. This is the real purpose of training. We were going to become soldiers to serve the country. So quite naturally, our training was tougher. The challenge of completing the training itself made us more keen to go through it. It inspired us to give our best shot at every step. For us, it was like a trial of fire. If we emerged unscathed, we would be doing justice to our uniforms.

I also knew that we would get our uniforms only after the training. Not only did I have to make myself worthy of the uniform, I knew that there was a pre-decided time for everything. I kept waiting for the glorious day and put up with the strictest regime because I wanted to earn it. So I did the training and work assigned to me every day as best as I could, always ready for new challenges.

After five months of training had passed, I got leave for twenty-eight days. Before I could go home, I had to sit for some tests. The training had been conducted by such capable people that I passed the tests easily.

Finally the day came when we were to proceed for our leave. I started making preparations from the morning itself. The train for Delhi was at 3 p.m. and we were to leave for the station at around 2.

Before leaving, we were asked to assemble in one place. We were asked whether we had eaten lunch and packed our dinner as well as a bottle of water. Now you know why I compared the Platoon Havaldar to a mother. We were told not to trust anyone or have any food offered by them. We were sent off with such pieces of advice. After that, an Ustad came to the station to see us off and saw to it that we got into the train and took our seats. I was feeling a bit relaxed now and knew the others would also be in the same state of mind. We started our journey with lots of laughter and jokes.

I noticed one thing at that time. There was a lot of difference in the jokes we had cracked earlier and those that we were sharing now. When we were going for the training, we had cracked jokes which seemed very immature now. The sort of jokes we shared now were more balanced.

It was the impact of the environment and ideals at the training centre that had infused in me a sense of self control along with a new passion for life. I can say without hesitation that all this was a result of the thorough training given by the Army. They had transformed a childish young boy to a responsible citizen of the country who understood life and its essentials.

When I came home on leave, I got a lot of love and affection from the members of my family. Since my elder brother was in the Army, as were some others in the village, everyone was aware of the strict regime during the training. So I was pampered quite a bit. My neighbours were amazed at the change that had come in me. They gave their children my example to follow.

It has been truly said that knowledge empowers a human being as it leads to self-awareness and social progress.

Knowledge is invaluable – whatever the source may be, wherever one might get it, in whatever form.

16

Rigorous Training

When I came home on leave for twenty-eight days, I had a lot of fun. I had a good time with my friends and family and also helped around with work in the fields. I was like a hero for everyone. My friends were delighted to take me along with them and the people of the village were very proud of me. I came to know that my friends had planned to do a number of things while I was there. My parents had also been looking forward to my visit, as they would receive some financial help from me as well.

During the journey towards home, we all reached the Delhi station. We all had to go our own way. For me, it was still a long way till home. First, I took a bus to my town. From the town bus depot, I hopped into a bus that went to my village. The home was quite far off from the bus stand, and I had to walk all the way. I stood on the side and opened my briefcase to dig the cap out, only to be stunned out of my wits. I had received five thousand rupees as remuneration during my training, which I had kept in a bag hidden inside my clothes. Now, that same bag was lying on top of my clothes, empty.

Sadly, my first salary could not reach home as it was stolen. I was very disappointed, but could do nothing about it. I did not say anything to anyone at home, but told them that I would get it only at the end of my training. I did not tell my friends as well. Everyone kept asking for a treat. But I just told them that I would throw a party for them the next time I came home.

Time flew by quickly. Along with enjoying myself, I also had to work in the field. By the time I had to get back, I had harvested the grain, husked it and even got the field ready for the next sowing.

When I left home, I had to tell my mother the truth. I confessed that I had no money, otherwise how would I travel back. 'All of it was stolen. That is why I could not give you anything.'

My mother lovingly stroked my head and chided me for hiding this from her and bearing its weight alone. She gave me a thousand rupees for my expenses and wished me luck.

I caught the bus to Delhi, where I met all the others who had come on leave with me.

All of us looked visibly sad. Some were remembering their parents while others were thinking of their girlfriends. I watched them, deep in my own thoughts. The train had already arrived at the station and we loaded our luggage onto it, ready for the ride back.

As soon as it was evening, we asked each other what food they had got from home. We were very hungry and most of us had extra food packed, in case someone needed it.

We put all the food in one place and shared it. It was magical to eat food together which was so lovingly made. We fell asleep, talking to one another and reached our destination at the crack of dawn.

A bus had come from the training centre to receive us.

Since I had just come from home, I was missing it acutely. I felt that the others were also lost in thoughts about their home and family. When the instructor came in the afternoon, he realized that we were still morose about coming from home, so he focused on us.

Do you know how young trainees are taught to get over the memories of home and family? We were made to lie down and roll all around our cots. A few moments later, we all were perspiring heavily. My clothes looked so dirty that it seemed they had been soaked in muddy water for ages. After sometime, they started dripping. That's when the Ustad said, 'Son, if you had cleaned the floor properly in the morning, the need to clean it like this would not have arisen.'

We realized what he was trying to say. But even after this, he made us do such strenuous exercises that we were totally exhausted. To tell you the truth, all our thoughts about home and family disappeared like magic.

♋

The very next day, we started with our advanced training. It did not seem even in the least bit that we had come back from home just the previous day. The fact that there was still four months' training left was enough to make us feel exhausted. I did whatever was assigned to me with full sincerity. I missed my home and family, but I did not let it come in my way where work was concerned.

I performed well and completed the hard training of three months. I was a member of the young firing team of the centre. New recruits who have the best aim are selected for this team. We would spend a great part of the day at the firing range, practising. We were severely punished if we missed the bull's eye. I understood that training us in this way was essential and could make a difference of life and death in the long run. So we also put in our best effort.

Sometimes we would be hit harshly for missing the target. However, we had been beaten up so much that being hit by the stick had barely any impact on us. I realized it was the slow and steady way of the Army to make us resilient to physical pain and small injuries. At such times, the Ustad would hit us on the legs or back and we would laugh.

One day, he was so irritated by our laughing that he cut a small electric cable and hit us with that. It hurt a lot and left a mark on our bodies. There were so many marks on our bodies that we made fun of each other while taking a bath that evening. But we took it as part of our training. These beatings were preparing us for difficult challenges in future. We were constantly reminded that a soldier has to complete his tasks, however difficult the circumstances might be.

We went on with our training with this mindset. Only a person who could see the intentions behind the Ustad's blows, instead of being cowed down by them, would become a brave soldier and serve his country well.

> *We are all destined to fulfil some role in this world. And we can do it if we burn ourselves in the fire of challenges and sharpen our skill. That will lead us to become a better version of us.*

17

The Festivities of My Brother's Marriage

Soon after, the training was complete. This was followed by a police verification. When we meet someone, it is up to us to leave a mark in their mind and heart with our deeds. which is mandatory before the next step. Some of my mates had completed the procedure already, and were through with the oath-taking ceremony.

It was around the end of October 1997. I got leave for about six days post the completion of the training. I was told to complete the formality of police verification within that period. I had to head back to my native place and do the needful there.

When I reached home, I was told that my elder brother's marriage had been fixed on 8 December. He was working with the Electronics and Mechanical Engineers Corps (EME) in the Army.

It was indeed a festive occasion for the family. After a very long time, there was something to celebrate. I helped everyone with the work as much as possible during those six days, alongside proceeding with the process of verification. As part of the process, I got the papers regarding verification from the police headquarters. Then I signed and sent them to the training centre by military postal service.

I was helping with the preparations for the marriage, and often wondered whether I would get leave again so soon. By now, members of my family had started urging me to get married as well.

When my mother asked me how many days before the marriage would I be coming home, I told her I might not be able to. Honestly, I did not know the process of asking for leave, so I said that I would not be able to come. In my mind, I thought that if indeed I was granted leave, I could always give them a surprise.

They said very confidently, 'We will call you.'

So I said casually, 'All right!'

After completing my leave, I reached the training centre, deposited the copy of my verification by hand in the office and took part in the oath-taking parade. Now, like my course mates, I was also a part of the Grenadiers. It was a moment of pride.

After months of rigorous training and hard work, I finally put on my uniform. I had dreamt about this right from my childhood. And at last, my wish had been fulfilled.

What came with the uniform was not just self respect, but a sense of onus as well. I was not just a trainee; I was a soldier. I had more responsibilities now. Till now, I had been assigned work fit for a recruit, but now I was assigned duties like a soldier. I put all my heart and mind in my duty because I had always been keen to learn new things.

In no time, it was December. Soon, it became clear how the members of my family had been so sure of calling me over for the marriage. They sent the invitation card of my brother's wedding at the address of the Centre. I had informed my seniors earlier that my elder brother was getting married. So the card was received without much fuss.

But within a few days, a telegram came, saying that my mother was seriously ill. I was worried because Maa was the one to take most stress so that could have led to something. But then, this was followed by a telegram which said that my father's condition was very serious.

Imagine that my seniors already knew about the marriage at home, and then these two telegrams arrived. All in all, the sequence of events portrayed me as a liar.

I tried to talk to my seniors and explain my perspective, but they would just not listen to me. They thought I was making all kinds of excuses to go home, even getting my family to send telegrams that carried a fake message. It could also set a wrong example in front of others, that they could do such antics and get away with it.

'Sir, I agree that the telegrams are false, but I honestly have nothing to do with them. There is a wedding at home and there is nothing fake about it,' I told my senior.

He retorted, 'The news of marriage is also false! All these are excuses and you will not be given leave. That's final!'

I knew that the matter was out of my control because of those false telegrams. I could make out what the senior officer's viewpoint was and it made perfect sense.

So I said, 'All right sir, I won't go. Not like the wedding won't happen if I don't go.'

I could not attend my brother's wedding. I really wanted to, but I was a soldier in the Indian Army and it was my first and foremost duty to obey the orders issued by the Army.

On 8 December 1997, which was the day of my brother's wedding, I had a good time with my friends. It seemed like I was attending the wedding. I was celebrating in my own way.

Eating, drinking and dancing were not allowed at the Centre during evenings. Everyone knew that. But when my friends noticed that I was somewhat sad, they got together and did not let me miss my family. We got punished by an Ustad who was angry that we had broken the rules, but that did not matter. All of us shared the punishment with the peace that we had celebrated on the day of my brother's wedding. I was assured more than ever that day that I was never alone.

For a soldier, the Army is his first family and the instructions issued from the seniors must be followed without fail. Familial happiness can never be given priority over those of the Army duties.

Even today when I tell my mother that the night of my brother's wedding was very special for me, she does not understand.

'But you were not even here!' she points out.

I feel that to be part of some festivity, one need not be present there physically. Wherever one might be, one can celebrate the event grandly. I felt bad at not being able to attend my brother's wedding, but I did not mope about it. On the other hand, I made the best of the situation. If I had attended the wedding physically, those memories would not have been created, which bring a smile to my lips even today.

> *If you ponder too much over things that are not in your control, you will miss creating many precious moments you have complete control over.*

18

Heading to my Unit

We heaved a sigh of relief when the nine-month training period was over. However, there was more training to be given after the oath-taking ceremony as well. After all, we had to be fully prepared to be in the Army.

All of us had been recruited together, so we were sent to our unit together too. We had shared everything at the training centre – good as well as bad experiences. It had been a wonderful journey of growth, resilience and love for the country. But now, after facing the rigours of training, it was time for us to part ways. We had been assigned to different units and we assured each other that now, we had to go to different homes and do our duty there.

Finally, after all the formalities were completed, on 31 December 1997, our Training Centre sent us off. Though we had faced some punishments and challenges here, for us, this

Centre was our first home on the new journey. I was a little sad at the time of leaving, but remembered that doing my duty and shouldering responsibilities was my priority. Moreover, the excitement regarding the future kept me going. We had a good time together the night before leaving as no one knew whether we would see each other again. The next morning, we wished each other well and left.

Two of my friends and I had been assigned to the same unit. It's a rule that one gets leave after finishing all the trainings, just before we report to our respective units. So we all were heading home for now.

All three of us had travelled to Delhi, and from there, we went towards our respective destinations. There was a lot of luggage as we had brought all our belongings from the Centre. We had to take help from porters to carry them to the bus stand. Finally, I got a bus in the evening. Only I know how difficult it was to load that entire luggage on the bus since I did not want to bother other passengers. Somehow I managed and got into the bus.

I did not get a place to sit, so I placed my military trunk straight up vertically and stood holding on to it. I was standing on one side so that passengers getting off did not face any problems. After going some distance, the bus stopped and a girl got in. She did not move forward towards the middle section, but sat down on the seat behind the conductor. I was also keeping an eye on the seats at the back to see if I could get a place to sit with my trunk. Then I would not cause any problem to other passengers.

Suddenly, I noticed that the girl was staring at me, as if trying to recognize me. Right then, an elderly man, who was standing close to the girl, called me by my name.

He said, 'Arre Yogendra, where have you got posted?'

I was taken aback. How did he know my name? Then I realized that my name was written on my trunk, something I had totally forgotten about. I looked hard at the elderly man, trying to see if I knew him. When I found that I did not know him, I wondered how he knew me.

I was still thinking if I should reply or not when the elderly man said, 'I saw your name on the trunk. That's why I called your name. My son is also in the Army.'

Now I knew that he was not known to me and felt reassured. I told him that I had got posted to Kashmir.

To my surprise, the girl continued to stare at me. I felt a strange kind of uneasiness at the way she was staring at me. I turned my back to her and looked the other way.

After about an hour, the bus stopped at the last bus stand on the route, my town. Everyone got off, except for me and the girl. I said to her politely, 'Madam, you should get off first. I have a lot of luggage.'

She also said, 'No problem. You go first!' She did not budge from her seat.

I said again, 'Please get off first. It will take time to unload my trunk.'

Anyway, she got down and waited outside, near the bus. I said, 'Madam please move away or you might get hurt by my luggage.'

She said firmly, 'I will not move from here.'

I was wondering why she was behaving so obstinately. So, I said, 'All right, don't move.' I told her, 'I am pushing the trunk down. Don't complain if it hurts you.'

She retorted, 'Just hurt me and then you will see!'

I did not pay much attention to her and pushed the huge metal trunk down. It was very heavy, full to the brim with my stuff. Then I and pushed the trunk out of the bus. Only then did she move away.

I unloaded the luggage one by one from the roof of the bus, and called for a rickshaw. Then I put all those things onto it and told the rickshaw-wala to go to the bus stand in my village. The girl was listening to my conversation with him. I got into the rickshaw and left. She continued to stand there.

By the time I reached the village bus stand, I had forgotten the incident, thinking only about taking all these things home. Somehow I managed to do it and reached my village. By the time I got home, it was post sunset, but I was very happy. It was wonderful to have food cooked by my mother after such a long time. Papa and my younger brother were also there and we talked about various things.

Then my mother said, 'Your bhabi was here till yesterday. Now she will come after a month. But she told me that you should go and meet her.' Maa smiled and told me to go and meet her.

I said, 'Maa, I don't know her or anyone else in her family. It does not seem proper for me to visit them all by myself.'

Maa said, 'Who will go with you? There's so much work around here all the time. You have to go on your own.'

I told her, 'Alright, I will take a couple of my friends and go with them.'

Mother told me not to take my friends with me and I refused to go alone.

When my father saw that we could not arrive at a solution, he said that the topic should be discussed the next morning. We went off to sleep after dinner. Papa told me they were planning to sow sugarcane the next morning.

He got up early and went to the field. An interesting thing about life in a village is that the sowing of sugarcane is carried out jointly by all members of the community. This is followed by a feast of *kheer*, *puri* and vegetables, which is partaken by all those who had helped in the sowing. That day too, there were about ten or twelve people working on the field, including me.

At about 11 in the morning, the sowing was completed. Right then, a young boy about the same age as my younger brother was seen coming towards our field. My cousin asked, 'Jitendra, how come you are here?'

Since my elder brother has the same name, I thought he had come home on leave. I looked back with excitement, only to find out that it was someone else. I asked my cousin who he was.

He said, 'This is Jitendra bhaiya's brother-in-law.'

He greeted me and said, 'Didi has called you.'

I had told my mother that I would not go alone to meet bhabi and I told him the same. He said, 'Go home and talk to your mother.'

I looked around and noticed that most of the work had been done, so I went home.' When I reached, I found out that Maa had already promised my bhabi to send me with her brother. When Maa told me this, I tried to resist, but she did not listen to me. Finally, I had to set off with him.

I said, 'I will go on one condition. You will come to drop me home. He agreed to this at once.

Their house was about ten kilometres from ours and we reached there soon enough.

I was hesitant in stepping into the house, since I was meeting everyone for the first time. As I stepped into the courtyard outside the house, I saw the same girl who had been staring at me in the bus.

I thought, 'This cannot be my bhabi!' It was more of a prayer, given my not-so-happy encounter with her.

With these thoughts, I stepped inside and wished her.

She asked me, 'Did you recognize me?'

Her tone was sharp, but I answered rather politely, 'Yes, I have.'

She said, 'I am your bhabi's elder sister. She has gone out for a bit. You sit. I will just call her.'

I went inside the room and sat there quietly. I was somewhat relieved that the girl in the courtyard was not my bhabi.

In those days, there was no mobile so I had nothing to divert my attention. I was getting bored, but soon, my bhabi came in. I greeted her and started talking to her. I observed that my bhabi and her sister weren't alike in their temperaments, which was a relief.

I had lunch with her where we had very interesting conversations. I was glad to know her more. After having food,

I said goodbye to everyone and came back home. This was the first time I had met my bhabi, which became the main event of my leave.

Before I realized, the one month leave was over. Time had just flown by. I had a good time sharing the work load in the house, meeting friends and having food cooked by Maa.

Most of the time, I was either in the field or at home. At home too, there was a lot of work to be done. I wanted to finish a few things quickly as I was not sure whether my mother and my younger brother would be able to complete them. So, I wanted to wrap up that work before leaving.

Finally, the day came when I had to leave for my Unit - 18 Grenadiers for the first time. My train was from Meerut that evening. I left home in the afternoon and carried food with me. I hopped on to the train that would take me to my Unit.

When embarking on new journeys, fear is natural. But hard work and dedication overcomes it with ease.

19

Reporting to the Transit Camp

I had to report for duty at Jammu on 8 February 1998. The bus for the transit camp was waiting at the station, but my friends and I decided to go for a haircut first. Our hair had grown long in the leave period and we had found out that the transit camp was close by.

To tell you the truth, that was perhaps the most expensive haircut I have ever had. For one thing, we were new to the city and the barber must have realized from our conversation that we were new jawans who had come to report for duty. Moreover, we had a lot of luggage and wanted to have our hair cut very short. So we had to pay whatever he asked for.

After the haircut, we reached the transit camp at nine in the morning. First, we deposited our documents and completed all the formalities. Then we were told to collect our winter uniforms.

It was February, so it was biting cold. We located the tent where we had to pick the uniforms from and reached there in a group. Naik Ranvir Singh was responsible for handing out the uniforms. There were three of us who were going on a new posting – Me, Sanjay Kumar and Anuj Kumar. The Naik asked us our names, the names of our village, district and state very courteously. Then he told us about 18 Grenadiers and issued us our winter uniforms and the rest of the things. He made a list of those items and made us sign it.

Till then, I had always written my name in Hindi, so I followed the same practice. The commander asked immediately, 'Up to which class have you studied?'

I said, 'Tenth.'

'Didn't you study English?'

'I have, sir.'

Surprised, he asked, 'Then why did you not sign in English?'

I scribbled my name in English right below the signature and did not give much thought to the matter. Maybe as the form was in English, I would have to sign it in the same language.

In the meanwhile, he started talking to us. He said, 'I have been working here for seventeen years. I have studied up to eighth standard and can sign in English.' In this way, he tried to impress us. We listened to his speech, standing quietly for about one-and-a-half hours and in the meantime, the formalities were completed. I was not sure when he would leave us! After all, we had to have our meal and leave for Srinagar the next morning.

Coming back home during holidays
also meant working on the fields.

Soon after joining the Army.

GETTING READY FOR BATTLE

Tough terrain; tougher Armymen

General V.P. Malik, the then Chief of the Army Staff, motivating soldiers of our Unit during the Kargil War.

With fellows, preparing for a tough battle ahead.

Prepping up battle weapons to win back captured territory.

Bringing the wounded soldiers back to the base camp.

WINNING BACK TOLOLING PEAKS

The Unit langar after the victory.

Col Khushal Singh Thakur, (now Brigadier, Retd), the Commanding Officer of 18 Grenadiers, addressing the media after winning Tololing.

THE HERO OF TIGER HILL

Braving the cold and all other odds in service of the country

Jawans atop the peaks,
in position.

Honoring heroes
who were killed in action.

The brave men of 18 Grenadiers with
their CO Col Khushal Thakur.

Enemy weapons captured at
Tiger Hill by 18 Grenadiers.

Our jawans and the tiranga atop Tiger Hill after a ferocious battle.

PARAM VIR CHAKRA

Honorable President
Sh K.R. Narayanan presenting the prestigious Param Vir Chakra to me.

My name was announced as the recipient of the Param Vir Chakra, while I was recovering in the hospital.

One of the pictures from my really long recovery time at the Army Hospital in Delhi.

FELICITATION BY THE ARMY

Rifleman Sanjay Kumar (Param Vir Chakra), Grenadier Yogendra Singh Yadav (Param Vir Chakra) and Lt Balwan Singh (Mahavir Chakra) *(left to right)*

With my Kargil war time CO Col Khushal Thakur.

I was conferred with the honorary rank of Captain by the Honorable President of India on 15 August 2021.

Lt Gen Rajeev Sirohi, Military Secretary and Colonel of the Grenadiers, presented the rank badges to me.

Statue at the National War Memorial in New Delhi.

Received much love on my superannuation in December 2021.

With my mother *(centre)*, wife *(right)* and sons.

NEW BEGINNINGS

After serving at the Junior Leaders Academy in Bareilly,
I am currently enjoying my role as a motivational speaker and change maker.

Photo credits:
Author, Archives of The Grenadiers Regiment and 18 Grenadiers,
public domain, DNA India digital post in July 2020.

Finally, he left us after a long lecture and told all three of us to stick together. He also said that a vehicle would be sent for us to take us to our unit.

After that long dose of *gyaan*, we finally had our lunch. Soon after, the Company Havaldar Major blew his whistle. Everyone was called and assigned numbers till ten at night and given the relevant documents. Some of us were asked to take weapons for the security of the bus and one person was made the commander of the bus. The Company Havaldar Major said, 'The bus will be kept ready at two in the night. Tomorrow, the bus will leave for Jainagar at 4 in the morning. If anyone is left behind, he will have to make his own arrangements.'

That alerted me immediately. I resolved to keep a watch on time, so that I did not miss the bus.

In those days, there were very few cots in the transit camps, and those too were mostly meant for seniors. The rest spread out their bed rolls and slept on it. With difficulty, I managed to sleep at 11:00 p.m., but was woken up by a commotion near us around 12.30. I saw that everyone was getting ready, waiting outside the toilet or brushing their teeth. Some were trying to wake their mates, others were going to fetch breakfast. Altogether, there was a lot of chaos.

I also woke my friends up. The place was so crowded that it was impossible for everyone to get ready at the same time. In all this commotion, if someone took something belonging to you by mistake, it would be impossible to get it back. So we had to take care of all these things while getting ready.

Once we had freshened up, we started searching for our bus. It took some time as there were many buses headed out into different directions. We found it after much looking, and put all our luggage on the carrier at the top. Then we went inside the bus and took our seats.

The bus was supposed to leave at 4 a.m., but we dare not sit anywhere else. What if we fell asleep and missed the bus and our luggage! So we sat on those cramped seats and slept uncomfortably in that situation.

Exactly at 4:00 a.m., the Havaldar blew his whistle. We assembled outside the bus. We were made to sit according to the order of our names and given instructions for the journey. The bus would stop at some places, but not on the route. Breakfast was to be provided at Ramvan, where the bus would stop for half an hour. After all these instructions, we all said in chorus, '*Bajrang Bali ki jai, Bhole Baba ki Jai, Bharat Mata ki Jai.*' With this, the bus set off for Srinagar.

Ripe fruits fall off the trees and touch the earth.
In the same way, knowledgeable people are
humble and down to earth.

20

The Journey from Srinagar to the Unit

9 February 1998

We reached Srinagar. It was evening when our bus reached the transit camp. The distance from Jammu to Srinagar was three hundred kilometers, which we covered in fifteen hours. It was not a short period which included long hours in daylight. Since we couldn't really sleep, we spent our time looking at the beautiful landscape and mountains all around us. I had heard from people and read in books about the breathtaking beauty of Kashmir. Isn't it why it is considered to be the 'heaven on earth'! I felt lucky to have had a first-hand glimpse of this heaven.

Such a heavenly place should be the abode of gods! I couldn't help but feel sad about how it had been sabotaged by demons in the form of terrorists. This was the abode of lord Shiva, so how was it possible that he had not opened his third eye and burnt them up!

I have always been a devotee of lord Shiva and thought that maybe Shiva had called us all there so that we, his devotees, could destroy these demons for him.

Lost in all these thoughts, we reached the transit camp in Kashmir. We unloaded our luggage one by one and assembled in one place. The Company Havaldar commanded us to line up. Duties were allocated for the night after the counting had been done. The seven of us jawans were assigned the duty of cooking in the *langar* for three days.

I said, 'Sir, we are new. Please tell us when the vehicle from our Unit will come and where we have to go.' This was because we had not received any instructions regarding further travel.

He said, 'You will be called when the vehicle from your Unit arrives. Don't worry!'

So we took our bedding and proceeded towards the langar. Our first task was to make laddus. The very mention of laddus made my mouth water. Just as we reached the cooking area, the Company Havaldar said in jest, 'Start your work quickly. You have to make laddus out of bigger coal chunks to be used for cooking.'

My mouth dried up at once. We had the duty for two hours that day and then, the next day as well. So we started our work of making balls of coal after our meal. It was only when we were done with the work that we got time to sleep. The bus journey of fifteen hours had been very tiring. We went off to sleep the moment our heads hit the bedding.

The next day, we got up early and the rest of the day was spent in doing work with fellows. In the evening, we met the cook of the langar, who is also known as the *khansama*. He asked us the name of our Unit. It turned out that he was also from our Unit. Meeting someone from our Unit felt like meeting a family member. Then we asked him when we were going to leave for the Unit, since we had not received any information regarding it as yet.

He probably read my mind, for he smiled and said, 'Don't be scared, I will take you along.'

This was reassuring. I was a little hesitant about where to go and how to do the required formalities. Back then, I was just eighteen years old and wanted someone to assure me, which this cook did with ease. Following that, the next two days were spent in working.

It was only after three days of our reaching the camp that the vehicles of all units arrived to take the soldiers. As I loaded my luggage onto my vehicle, I felt that it was time for me to go to my real home.

If you look at it this way, the Unit is like home for the soldier where he goes as soon as his life in the Army starts. He spends all his youth there. With the same fervour, I stepped into the vehicle. It took about a couple of hours for us to reach the Unit. Getting down, we presented our identity cards and other documents to the Subedar Adjutant. He checked them all and sent us to our company.

In our Unit, there are four companies. Sanjay, Anuj and I proceeded towards B Company, which had been assigned to us.

The Havaldar Major of the company welcomed us when we reached. The company was further divided into platoons. I was sent to 5 Platoon and Sanjay and Anuj were sent to 6 Platoon.

The Platoon Havaldar welcomed me warmly and said, 'Son, wash your hands and feet. Then go to the store where you will be given some clothes for winter.'

I did as directed and went to the store. There, I was given two big white snowshoes. I also received many other things which I took. Then a senior Naik of the platoon said, 'You have arrived at the right time! Liquor will be served from today. You register yourself and get your ration. We will all celebrate together.'

I was very happy to hear this. I got my name registered there and asked for liquor. As soon as I had spoken, the Naik Subedar sitting there exploded, 'For whom have you come to take it? What is your name? When did you join the platoon?'

The questions came like blows, one after another. I answered each one politely. 'Sir, I have just arrived here. No one has asked me to get it. I want it for myself.'

I did not want to take the name of the senior, so I kept on saying that I wanted it for myself. But he would not relent.

Finally, he said, 'All right, if you want it for yourself, you will have to sit here and drink it.'

If I had to save my neck on the very first day in the platoon, I had to find a middle way. What else could I do!

I said, 'All right sir.'

He poured two pegs into my glass and started pouring water.

I said, 'Sir, I won't take water.'

I picked up the glass and gulped down the two pegs in it. He smiled and said, 'You are a *pakka* drinker. When did you start drinking?'

Then I told him that my father had been in the Army. He used to get liquor for himself. He would ask me to make a peg and I would make myself one too, pouring water in the bottle to cover it up.

When I told him I had first tasted alcohol when I was in the sixth standard, he was quite surprised. He asked me curiously, 'Do your brothers also drink as much?'

I said, 'No sir, none of them drink.'

He let me go after this brief conversation. I reported the events and how they had unfolded to the senior, and then came back to my room and slept.

The next morning, I came to know that there were a few senior jawans and one Havaldar from a village close to mine, and one from my own village. By now, all of them knew that there was a boy from their village, who was a pakka drinker.

What I had said jokingly, had earned me the fame of a certain kind in my Unit. While you might feel that I was infamous, I believe that it was something people laughed about *with me.* That helped me build strong bonds from the very first day in the Unit. This was a journey I was never going to forget.

When we meet someone, it is up to us to leave a mark in their mind and heart with our deeds.

21

The Style of Working in the Unit and the Way it Functions

At the time of my arrival, the unit was conducting a pre-induction training in Srinagar. My team mates and I also became a part of that training. We were enlightened about how terrorists operated, how they attacked armed buses, which groups were active in our area and how many commanders led these terrorist outfits. We were also trained on how to interact better with the civil administration and the general public.

I realized that this training was meant to enable us to build a goodwill towards the general public. Along with this, we were responsible for eliminating the terrorists in our area. But before all that, my first priority was to win the confidence of other jawans as well as the people of the area. We should be able to connect ourselves with the new environment and feel at home there. I concentrated on my training.

I knew that the best way of knowing others better would be to ask more questions – which I did. I knew that there were many kinds of troublemakers in Kashmir who were always trying to incite the public against the Army so that their work became easier. So I had resolved to win the confidence of the people and only then proceed further.

I firmly believe that whatever work is done sincerely, always leads to success. I won the confidence of my mates and seniors in the platoon with my hard work and firm resolution. I was always ready to work because I really considered the platoon my second home. I respected my elders and loved my fellow soldiers in the platoon in the same way as one would do at home.

I did not have much work at home except cleaning up the courtyard and filling drinking water in the pitchers. It was the same tradition in the Army. The junior jawan had to do all the work in the platoon. Since I was used to doing all this work at home already, it did not seem like a burden to me.

The first duty of a jawan was to get a kettle of tea from the langar and serve the entire platoon. After this, he was supposed to clean the area in the platoon and fill drinking water in the pitchers. It is true that one does not join the Army to do all this, but this was work, not punishment. Moreover, this was a time-tested way in which the new jawan could win the support of all and later receive their cooperation. This was very helpful in infusing a spirit of teamwork in the platoon.

If the platoon functions like a good team, it would compete with other platoons in standards of excellence. In my personal opinion, whenever platoons compete with each other, the Company is sure to reach peaks of excellence. It is to keep up with this work culture that a new jawan is made to do all this work.

Along with this, the Platoon Havaldar is able to judge the jawan's skills, efficiency and capability. One can also evaluate the physical as well as mental strength of the jawan doing all this work. His attitude also indicates his behaviour, ideas and mindset.

My behaviour, meticulous approach and growth mindset made me an irreplaceable part of my platoon. This was the first step of success in my professional career.

After one month's training, the Unit was posted in Kashmir. There too, the company was deployed to different villages. Every company had a different area of responsibility. Our company was deployed in a government school in a village.

Major Rajesh Adhikari was the Company Commander and Captain I.R.S. Rathore was the 2IC[5]. In their leadership, the company had different teams led by experienced Havaldars, Subedars and Naib Subedars. All of them were engaged in serving the general public in the area assigned to them, winning their confidence as well as finding out who was supporting the terrorists.

---

5. Second-in-command.

This work continued for a few months and our company was quite successful. As a result, terrorists could not move around as freely. Seeing this, we made our work our daily routine. Sometimes, we had to spend the whole day or night outside the camp. I agree that it was a rigorous regime, but I had started enjoying it and made it an integral part of life.

22

A New Chapter in Life Starts

Deployed in different parts of Kashmir, every company of the Unit was trying to fulfill its responsibility to the fullest. We were assigned a variety of tasks – the security of Army vehicles, election duty or looking after the security of Amarnath pilgrims. The Unit did all this in the best possible way. We worked with a motto to make living simpler for the locals, give security to those visiting the valley and curb the activity of the anti-social elements. With this three-pronged approach, we fulfilled our duties with utmost sincerity and dedication.

In this way, time passed. It was now 1999. New jawans like us were given two months leave at the beginning of January. I remember when I met the Company Commander Major Rajesh Adhikari, he smiled and asked, 'For how long are you going home on leave?'

I said, 'Sir, I am going for two months.'

He said, 'Take leave for thirty days, I am telling you. Otherwise you will come back and ask for leave again to get married.' He was smiling.

I said clearly, 'No sir, I don't want to get married right now.'

The matter ended there with mutual smiles and eventually, we set off for home. I did not know then that this leave was about to change many things in my life.

When I reached home in January 1999, it was terribly cold. But it did not bother me much as I had come back from Kashmir – where it was unbearably cold. The members of my family welcomed me very warmly. They asked me many questions and served me my favourite dishes. Like the previous time, I was pampered and given much love and respect by everyone in the community.

On my part, rather than whiling away my time, I helped with the work in the field, moved around with my friends and caught up with what had been happening. Even though I was rather young, many marriage proposals came for me. At first, I could not understand the reason. Why would someone want to marry their daughter to such a young, inexperienced boy? Then I realized that I had a government job, so people around us thought I was well-settled.

The scene hasn't changed much for people in villages even now. To this day, if a young boy gets a job, people try to marry him off. If the boy's family refuses for some reason, the word goes round that they want a hefty dowry.

I admit that in western Uttar Pradesh and Haryana, the dowry problem is deep-rooted and can cripple girls' families monetarily. Even the way in which it is demanded is unique. The boy's family says, 'We ask only for a rupee. But if you give your daughter any more than that, we will accept it humbly.' In such a situation, the girl's family has to guess what is in the minds of the boy's family.

All this is true, no doubt, but there are families that conduct marriages without any such transactions. I personally vouch for such relationships as they are built on strong foundations. Someone who is offering his daughter, the pride of his family, should not be asked for anything more.

Anyway, after considering a number of marriage proposals, my father shortlisted one. I wasn't giving him any positive response on this discussion, so he took charge of the matter and finalized a meeting. The girl's family came to 'see' me.

That morning, I had gone to the field to get fodder for the cattle. When my bullock cart reached in front of the house, my elder brother's childhood friend came to me and said, 'The girl's family is here to meet you.'

He was the one who had arranged the alliance. The girl in question was his wife's cousin - Reena. Today, the same girl is my wife.

But back then, this friend said, 'Get ready quickly and come to the terrace.'

I looked at myself. I was fully covered with mud. I washed myself with water from the tap in front of the kitchen and went up to the terrace. There were a few people sitting there – the girl's grandfather, father and uncle, along with one or two people from their village.

I said namaste to everyone and sat down with them. I guess they had been waiting for me only, because they started asking questions almost immediately. I answered them one by one, to the best of my ability. It was like an interview. When they had finished, they talked among themselves in soft voices. Then Papa told me to complete the rest of my work around home. I came down and went to Maa.

It must have been a few minutes when Maa asked me to take tea for everyone. I offered them tea and snacks and sat with them on Papa's insistence.

After they had finished their tea, the girl's uncle called me aside and asked, 'What car do you like?'

I looked straight at him and said, 'Uncle, I don't have such wishes. On this earth, no one can fulfill the desires of another person. Everything is in the hands of god. I cannot even drive a car, what will I do with it! I can only ride a cycle.' I said this, wished him and went back to help Maa.

I don't know what conversation they had with my father after I left. After two days, I came to know that my marriage had been fixed with that girl on 5 May.

Imagine my situation – it was like a typical Bollywood movie. I had not even seen the girl yet, leave aside talking to her. But that was the way things were done in our village.

Soon, it was time for me to go back. Though the leave was fairly long, I felt it had ended too soon. Maa and Papa bade me farewell happily, saying over and over that the next time I came, it would be time for the wedding.

I reached the Unit after a long journey once again. When I went to join formally, I met the Company Commander and told him the truth. 'Sir, I just got back from home. But I have something important to share with you.' He watched me quietly as I updated him, 'Sir, the date for my wedding has been fixed. It's on 5th May.'

He looked at me in the eye and said at once, 'I had told you, hadn't I? You should have taken leave for thirty days instead of sixty! Now, for how long will you take leave in May?'

I didn't have any answer. I said, 'Give me leave for twenty days, sir. That would be enough.'

He simply nodded and told me he would consider it. After that, all of us got busy with the work assigned to us. I had still not seen even a photograph of the girl who I was to marry. Since there used to be no mobile phones back in those days, there was absolutely no question of talking to her. I just imagined what she would be like. This one thought was of some solace in the hope of seeing her sometime soon.

Hope and faith are marvellous things. They help you through uncertainty and the darkest of times.

23

Contribution to the Unit in Kashmir

The Unit moved to different parts of Kashmir with the essential task at hand – to maintain law and order in the valley. We would patrol day and night, work very hard, but for the first eight to nine months, we did not have any success. We often heard news from other units – how they had killed so many terrorists, but we had still not gotten a chance to come face to face with any terrorist group.

We realized it had been a really long time and our efforts had not been any less. We were giving the task our heart and soul, but to no avail. Finally, we all started looking into the reasons for this – why we were not able to find any terrorists? It couldn't be that there were no such elements in the area. Maybe our intelligence network was not efficient enough. The only way forward seemed like a simple thing – we would have to win the confidence of the locals. It was a well-known fact that in Kashmir, terrorists could not operate without local sources or support, so our work would be very difficult without the support of locals.

Fighting terrorism in Kashmir is a different kind of battle because the enemy wears the dress of the locals, speaks their language and stays amidst them. It is challenging to distinguish between the terrorists and the local people. It is a difficult task for the Army as well, especially because people cannot cooperate out of fear. On the one hand you have to look after the security of the local people, and on the other hand, you have to eliminate the terrorists.

After being with the Unit for nine months, and numerous fruitless attempts, our battalion conducted a 'Cordon and search operation' in a village. That was when we ended up fighting terrorists for the first time. I remember that I had just come back from leave and the operation was launched the night after. In that operation, I had carried out a rocket launcher.

That fateful evening, three teams each from different companies were sent to the village. By two at night, we had surrounded the whole village. When it was morning, Lt. Col R. Vishwanathan, 2IC of the company, led us.

He had an announcement made from the mosque in the village. 'All the villagers should come out of their houses. The Army will search the village.'

No sooner had the announcement been made, firing started from the houses right next to the mosque. This was the first time I was seeing a live encounter in my career. Firing carried on from both the sides. Slowly, we got all the people out of the village. The terrorists had left the house they had fired from, but we were unable to spot the exact place where they were hiding now. It took us an entire day to look for them. Different teams were formed for the purpose as we had to look into each and every house. Despite our best efforts, we could not find a single trace of the terrorists.

It was evening. During the search operation, some of our jawans started looking into a heap of hay that was piled up in front of a house. Suddenly, the terrorists hiding in that pile started firing at us blindly. Two jawans from my unit were killed in their firing.

We managed to kill the terrorists, but had to pay a heavy price in the bargain. For three days, we held our ground there, not letting anyone go back to the village. We had arranged for food and resting place for the villagers while the operation went on.

There were perhaps some commanders among the terrorists, who were still in hiding. For the terrorists too, the commanders hold a higher place in the hierarchy. So there was a lot at stake if that turned out to be the case here. For three days, they continued to remain in hiding in the village. But now, they had run out of food, and their other resources were also dwindling. They now wanted to come out of their hiding and go to a safer place.

We were prepared to catch the terrorists, but we would have put a lot of lives at stake in the process. It had already been three days that these people were out of their homes, so the senior Army officials decided to step back for the moment.

It was disappointing, since we hoped to catch the remaining terrorists. But we retreated back to the Unit after helping the village people get on with their routine.

Two days later, in a separate operation, our Unit eliminated the top terrorist commander code-named Babar and his three comrades. This was our way of paying them back for killing our fellow jawans.

In a way, that episode broke the spell for our Unit. Where once we were not having any luck in our operations, after this particular event, wherever we went for an operation, we managed to eliminate terrorists. In the beginning, our Unit also had casualties; we lost some of our comrades. But learning a lesson from them, we conducted many cordon and search operations. We achieved a lot of success and our unit became well known. It will always be a matter of pride for me to be a part of this Unit and Platoon.

I wondered if our small steps and assistance would change the fate of the people of Kashmir. Then I realised, we were changing the world for them, slowly but steadily. And that was enough motivation.

PART – III

THE KARGIL WAR

24

The Problems of Kashmiri Locals

I must confess, Kashmir is a very beautiful place. But like all magnificent things, it had to be saved from the evil eye. Like I said, I kept asking seniors and fellows about the situation around, and somehow felt bad for the people in Kashmir. While carrying out our operations, when we conducted a search operation in a village, it was our first priority to look after the security of the civilians. So at the beginning of any operation, the people of the village were asked to leave their houses and assemble at a safe place. We made arrangements to set up resting places for older people, women and children. There was also medical assistance and food for everyone, considering they were out of their houses. Then we searched all the houses with the help of a few residents of that village who were known to us.

If the village was small, the search would be over by the evening. If the village was a big one and there were chances of encounters with terrorists, the operation could continue for two to three days as well. In that period, looking after the safety and well-being of the elderly people, women, sick people and children was the first priority of the Army.

We often felt this exercise took up a lot of time, and asked villagers to help us. They were polite with us and respectful, but there was an overwhelming sense of fear of the terrorists. These antisocial elements were well known to eliminate entire families if anyone as much as breathed against them. Which is why the Army had to be doubly careful about these operations.

The citizens of Kashmir have full faith in the Army, but their fear has become the ruling element in everyday life.

Since people were in such a pitiable condition, we tried our best to carry on our operations and eliminate terrorists without harming them.

At the very beginning of my career, I noticed that the factors which help terrorism to spread are still there. I am sure you understand that everything in this world needs a certain condition to flourish in. In my opinion, these are the things that help terrorism in the valley:

1. Help and assistance from local sources
2. Geographical conditions which provide them with hideouts
3. Money
4. Escape routes and ample resources.

These four factors are active even today. I sincerely believe, if their funding is stopped, not just Kashmir, but the whole world can be free of terrorism. I also know that it is impossible, because as we are moving towards progress, people are becoming selfish and concerned only with their own interests. A large section of the society has been left behind in this race of development. It has become increasingly difficult for them to look after themselves, their family and children.

We come to this world as human beings, but as we grow up, we change our lives in accordance with what we see and hear around us. Slowly, ideas of caste, creed, religion, country, poverty and affluence form in our minds. As they go deep into our subconscious mind, they give rise to certain thoughts. And gradually, our behaviour is shaped by these thoughts. These ideals and the behaviour determine the way we function.

Tell me something! If the common man has always heard of ways to cater to one's selfish interests, seen such people rise up faster the social ladder faster, how will he ever think of others?

Now, the situation is such that the entire atmosphere is coloured by selfishness and hatred. The social injustice is widening the gap between the rich and the poor. These are the differences that help terrorists to flourish.

You could say I am wrong, but I have seen this at very close quarters in Kashmir. I saw how youth were led astray in the name of religion and jihad. Many people are not aware of the fact that the Indian Army is conducting an operation in Kashmir called *Sadbhavna* (literally, good will). With the help of this, several school children are taken on educational tours to different parts of the country. The purpose of this is to acquaint them with the mainstream atmosphere of the country. Sadly, Kashmir is not really the ideal place to start with, which is why exposure is necessary. These children are made to realize that the country extends from Kashmir to Kanyakumari, and from Gujarat in the west to the Northeastern states in the east. The feeling is instilled in them that all of it belongs to us and we have to take care of it. There will be a change only when they learn to treat the entire country as their own and dream of taking it to great heights.

During this Operation Sadbhavna, sports events are also organized across schools. In order to bring out the talent in children, it is important to find new avenues and this is one of them. We encourage Kashmiri youth to join the armed forces so as to make sure that they are not trapped by religious fundamentalists. Their contribution towards service for the nation would make it possible for the upliftment of their family as well as the state in the long run.

♋

I remember when we were posted in Kupwara, we were entrusted with the responsibility of preparing jawans for the Army. We called youth from surrounding areas and started the task to prepare them for the written and physical tests. During that period, when we asked them if they had ever been to Pakistan, many young men said that they had gone there a number of times, escorted by a boy from their village. In the initial days, I would ask in a surprised manner, 'Were you not scared to go to Pakistan?'

Their answers amazed me all the more. 'No sir. That boy knows the places where the Army is stationed and also those places from where we can get into a Pakistani village without being detected. He knows some Pakistani soldiers very well. No one said anything to him.'

Perhaps he realized from my reaction that I was surprised, so he added dramatically, 'Sir, AK 47 rifles are available there as openly as ration here.'

This was a group of five boys, out of which one was selected for the Army. Kashmiri boys were usually scared to join the Army because there were one or two terrorists in every village. As soon as they find out that a boy from a particular family had joined the Army, they start troubling other members of the family. This was a big reason for the youth to not step forward and join the forces, even if they wished to.

The boy who was recruited would spend most of his time in the unit, even when he was on leave.

The people in these areas danced to the tunes of the terrorists. Apart from the fear that the terrorists put in them, they also helped locals with money.

One night, while patrolling, we disguised ourselves as terrorists and went to a village. We knocked on a door and an elderly person opened it. There were four or five of us and one of them knew the local language. The elderly person made us sit in an inner room and started arranging for food. By that time, all the members of the family had woken up and started talking to us as if we were their close relatives. They looked after us very well the whole night and told us to leave at about four in the morning. We came back.

The next afternoon, after a gap of a few hours, we went to the same house, this time in our Army uniform. We asked the elderly man who opened the door, if anyone had come there the previous night.

The same man refused at once and vowed in the name of god that no one had come to their house the previous night. We realized how they were to scared to say anything !

This mindset is dangerous for peace and progress of humankind. When people realize the difference between right and wrong in the society and stand up against what they know is wrong, this evil will be destroyed automatically. In Kashmir too, religious fundamentalists have sown the seeds of hatred in the minds of some misguided youth and filled the rest of the people with fear. In such a situation, how can there be peace?

♋

I often used to wonder how nature has not made us with any differences. We are all essentially the same. It is us humans who have drawn lines of division all through the world.

Once I was sitting at a post with my friends. There were some monkeys there as well. Below the post, at a distance of two or three kilometres, was a village which fell in Pakistan. At that time of the year, corn was being grown there. I noticed that a monkey went down, broke a cob of corn from the field and came up. He sat near us and started eating it. I thought about how the monkey had gone to the field, falling in a different country and come back with a cob of corn to this country to eat it, without a care in the world.

I also noticed a river flowing nearby, which flowed from India to Pakistan. The water in the river did not know through which country it was flowing. It only knew that it should take the direction which could help the earth flourish the most. So it flowed on.

Birds fly thousands of kilometers to reach a place where the weather suits them best. They fly on, knowing nothing about borders. Man is perhaps the most intelligent creature on this earth. And yet, it is he who encourages racism, nationalism, colonialism and expansionism in order to fulfill his selfish desires.

This is what makes them kill others who are weaker or subjugate them, in order to rule over them. This kind of ideology is so influenced by selfishness that it blinds people who believe in it. One starts thinking that it would always remain the same and he would continue to rule over the country forever. But that is not true. Whatever is born in this world, has to fall from power or die one day. But the world goes on. Everything created by nature – rivers, mountains and streams – remains unchanged. If we keep this in mind, our actions are bound to benefit our own country at large.

> *When we make up our minds to complete a task, we won't stop short of achieving our goals. No matter what challenges come your way, build your inner strength to beat all odds.*

25

India became a Nuclear Power

Our former President, Bharat Ratna Dr A.P.J. Abdul Kalam was a patriot whom the whole world knows and respects. With his spiritual strength, skills and capabilities, he gave India the missile which has enabled her to stand on an equal footing with other powerful nations of the world.

In 1998, under the leadership of Kalam, India conducted the first nuclear test. Coincidentally enough, Pakistan conducted it at the same time. With that, both the neighbouring countries were equipped with nuclear power now.

Shri Atal Bihari Vajpayee, the then Prime Minister of India, had a very positive outlook towards politics and growth in general. He encouraged the Army and gave it moral support. He also congratulated the whole country for a successful nuclear test. Of course, a positive attitude has its own place, but reality is different. If two neighbouring countries do not share an amiable relationship, neither of them would be able to attain success at an optimal level.

Atal Bihari Vajpayeee extended a friendly hand to the Pakistan Prime Minister Nawaz Sharif in keeping with the Indian tradition. He started talks in order to put an end to terrorism in Kashmir, primarily so that both countries could move forward on the path of progress and development. This was welcomed by the people in both countries whole-heartedly.

In this context, a train named Samjhauta Express was started between the two countries, along with a bus between Delhi and Lahore. Our Prime Minister himself travelled by this bus and showed the world that India wanted a peaceful relationship with her neighbour. He made it amply clear that India was interested in the progress of the neighbouring countries along with her own. We were willing to lend them a helping hand in the process.

India knows how to respect and honour humanity. We have always worked, keeping the human interest as our topmost concern. Both countries progressed in the field of foreign policy and military strategy as a result of these small but significant steps.

The successful nuclear test boosted the morale of the Army as well, with the thought that it would empower it better. And why not, every soldier wants his country to become powerful and self-reliant. He wants his country to be at the top of the world in every aspect. He is ready to sacrifice himself for the honour of his country. He wants to see his country at the height of power and as a strong nation. Every soldier wants to create the kind of atmosphere in the country in which people can live without fear and work confidently towards attaining great progress and excellence.

If every person in the country thinks like a soldier and has feelings of nationalism within him or her, nothing can stop the country from being at the peak of success. Every person in the country should be as conscious of his or her duties as the rights. The soldier posted at the border thinks not only of protecting his fellow citizens, but also promoting peace within the country.

The country can be defended not only with the help of arms and ammunition, but also by promoting internal strength, which comes from unity. This is what Dr Kalam, also known as the Missile Man of India, did. By enhancing the nuclear power in the country, he forced our enemy countries to bow before us. What we had achieved by our talent, capability and skill increased not our pride.

There's one more thing that I have always firmly believed in. The security of the country does not depend only on one organization. The thinking that only the Army is responsible for the security of the nation is wrong. The citizens of the country should also contribute to it by doing their duty in the best possible manner. However, when a country progresses, other countries consider it as a threat and try to block it.

The ideology of the nation is made up of the thoughts of the people living there. When a person feels jealous at the prosperity of his neighbour, it is natural for a country to feel envious of the prosperity of the neighbouring country.

Every developed country tries its best to stop countries around it from progressing. This is done to retain supremacy and ensure that other nations remain dependent on it.

In order to grow as a person, you must ensure the betterment of everyone around you.

26

Reasons behind the Kargil War

Prime Minister Atal Bihari Vajpayee was having talks with the Prime Minister of Pakistan Nawaz Sharif in order to bring about a friendly relationship between the two countries. The people in both the countries were feeling relaxed, thinking that these talks would sort out the differences between the two countries. There were conscious attempts to revive business relations between the two countries. Those with relatives across the border thought it would give them a chance to solidify personal relations with them.

But some extremists, who were in power in Pakistan, did not want the relations between the two countries to improve. This was because they thought that their fundamentalist ideas and inhuman attitude would be curbed if such an atmosphere prevailed. So they got together and conspired in such a sinister manner that was beyond one's imagination. While the majority of people in both the countries thought that the fifty-year-old conflict would come to an end, these people had something up their sleeve.

The fundamentalists in powerful positions scrutinized the vulnerable points of India. They were clever enough to keep in mind their position and the way in which they themselves would be safe, even if some action was taken by India. So they chose an area where there had been no conflict earlier; nor did the Indian Army expect any problems in that region.

General Pervez Musharraf, the then Pakistan Army Chief, chose Kargil after a lot of planning. It was such a cold area that it was quite tough to hold posts there during winter. As per an earlier bilateral understanding, both armies were supposed to be in their base camps during winters, only to take positions atop the hills when summer arrived.

As a result, Musharraf knew very well that the Indian Army would be at the base camp. He also knew they would never break the understanding reached in the agreement. The Indian Army would leave their base camp and go atop when it was time. This was the best opportunity to capture the Indian posts, currently lying vacant.

He collected all the war material required in the next few months so that when the Indian Army came there early in the months of summer, it would be easy to stop them. He thought that he would easily annex these areas and make them a part of Pakistan. This was the plan to ruin any good efforts being made for peace in the nations. He must not have realized how bloody a war it was going to turn out.

In this way, he made a complete plan and deployed the new battalion of 45 Northern Light Infantry to Drass-Kargil-Batalik. As planned, they captured all the posts in the Indian territory during winters. Both India and its Army remained unaware of this encroachment, as this had been the norm for years following a bilateral agreement. In the meantime, Pakistan collected a lot of war material at all these posts. If it came to fighting, they could continue for quite a few months with ease.

So while Indian leaders, media and people felt glad at the Lahore–Delhi bus service continuing with gusto, Musharraf went behind everyone's back, collecting all kinds of arms, ammunition and food supplies on the peaks of Kargil.

The enemy might be very shrewd, but the people of the country do love their own land. There are always people in these areas who wish to see India prospering. It is because of this goodwill, loyalty and love that I am sure no one can colonise our land or even think of grabbing it.

When the snow melted a little, the shepherds in that area went up the hills to graze their goats and sheep. They noticed people at Indian posts. They gave the information to the officers at base camps immediately.

At first, nobody was ready to believe that there were some other people at the Indian posts. When the same thing was confirmed by a few others and the Indian Army came to know all the details, they sent a team of 4 Jat, led by Captain Saurabh Kalia for patrolling and looking into the matter.

When they went up for patrolling, information was awaited at the base camp. But since the weather had also not yet completely cleared, there was no saying how long it would take them. But there was no news from them for a few days. Fearing that something had conspired, another team was sent to find out what had happened to the patrolling party. A few members of the second team were killed in action too, but some of them managed to come back and updated the officers at the base camp. They informed about the presence of enemy at the post. The news spread like wildfire that there were terrorists on the mountains of Drass-Kargil-Batalik.

Our senior officials planned a strategy to fight them and the task of eliminating them started. From April 1998 onwards, the mountains of Drass, Kargil and Batalik resounded with the noise of gunfire and bombs. The beautiful landscape was covered with blood.

No soldier ever wants a war. But when someone attacks his motherland, he would not stop short of laying down his life and fighting till the last drop of blood in his body.

27

The Beginning of Kargil War

In April-May 1999, as the winter months ended, terrorist activities increased multifold in the Kashmir valley. During that year, our Army was increasing its operations for the elimination of the terrorists in the valley. Specifically in the Kargil, Drass and Battalik sectors, the Indian Army was engaged in fighting the Pakistan army. At that time, the number of soldiers deployed in that mountainous area was less, as is standard during peace time. But all those who were there, gave the enemy a good fight. The situation demanded that more soldiers be sent to the area.

Our battalion was also called to Kashmir. At that time, we were engaged in anti-terrorist operations in different parts of the valley. During those months, our battalion had killed many feared terrorist commanders. In view of the disciplined and brave achievements, the higher authorities of our unit commanded that we should be sent to Drass.

When the unit received the command, I was in my village on leave. It was the time of my marriage ceremony. Some other members of my unit, from different companies, had also come home on leave. I had invited them to my marriage as well, since they were the only ones from my work front who could attend the festivities. Some of them had been my constant companions. Yogendra Singh, Mukesh Yadav, Dinesh Yadav and others were my good friends.

The marriage was solemnized on 5 May, and was attended by my friends. It was a sheer stroke of luck that they could be present for my big day. Since everyone does not get leave at the same time, only a few soldiers are able to attend a colleague's marriage. I had not been able to attend my brother's marriage as I did not get leave. It was a matter of good fortune that on that auspicious occasion, they could be by my side.

After the wedding festivities, my friends reached the Unit before me. The day after my wedding, an atmosphere of joy prevailed in the whole family. My friends and brothers kept on teasing me, making the atmosphere light and cheerful.

The same night, I had a dream that someone was running away with our national flag. Our soldiers were chasing him and some people were incessantly firing at them. Though they were wounded and full of blood, they still ran till their last breath, in order to save the national flag. They sacrificed themselves for the flag by the time the dream ended.

With that jarring thought, I woke up in the middle of the night. I also experienced a strange feeling of restlessness. I spent the rest of the night feeling uneasy.

Early the next morning, I told my parents and elder brother about the dream. Since Papa and Bhaiya had experienced the soldier life, they could understand the impact of my dream on my subconscious mind. But as a family, they did not make much of it then, as there was still an atmosphere of peace and hope in the country. Moreover, I had been married for just a day and they wouldn't have wanted to bring in any sense of gloom. Till then, there had been no reports of these encounters in the Kashmir valley in the newspapers, radio or on the television. But I had a strong apprehension that something was not right on the borders.

This was the time when harvesting and threshing was going on. Our relatives, who had come over for the wedding, left the day after the marriage. My brothers and I got busy on the field. In three or four days, we managed to store the grain as well as the fodder at home. Then we got busy with preparing the field for the next sowing. Since Bhaiya and I had just a few days of leave left, we thought we would prepare the field before leaving. This would make the work lighter for Maa and our younger brother. If this major task was done, they could manage the sowing with ease. So we were busy day and night. But my apprehensions would not leave me. They continued to bother me constantly, like an arrow stuck in my body.

My leave was about to come to an end. The whole time was spent in farming work so that no one faced any problems after we left. Soon it was the last day of my leave. In the morning, I got up and packed my belongings, putting in some sweets which my mother had made at home for me to take for my friends.

I had to leave by two in the afternoon to catch the Shalimar Express from Meerut in the evening.

It is the tradition in our family that one should leave after taking blessings from the elders and giving something to the younger ones in the family. When I left, I gave a hundred rupees to my wife and took the blessings of my parents and elder brother. Everyone wanted to know when I would come home next. Now there was one more person asking me the same question – my wife. I had no answer, so they asked me to write a letter as soon as I reached the Unit.

I reassured everyone that I would write to them. My elder brother saw me off at the bus stop. I reached Meerut that evening, boarded my train and left for Jammu. Maa had packed some food for the way, which I had and went off to sleep.

The next morning, when we reached Jammu and then the transit camp, the names of some jawans from several units were being called out. I heard it being announced that all those jawans who had come back from leave were to submit their papers at once and get ready to go to Srinagar. I did not understand why there was such a rush. On asking, I came to know that war had broken out in Kargil and our unit was a part of it. As soon as I heard this, I remembered my dream.

I had always hoped to fight for my country. Finally, that long-cherished dream was coming true. There was a lot of talk about the war and the morale of the jawans was very high. Some were sad, but others like me had hardly slept at night because of the adrenalin rush. We were ready to board the bus as early as four in the morning. We loaded our luggage onto our buses and were lost in the thoughts of what awaited us in the future.

In the evening, we reached the Srinagar transit camp and heard the names of units being announced. I submitted all my documents and started for Kargil the next morning itself. In the evening, my comrades and I reached Dumri, where the base camp of the unit was set up. We took our weapons and the rest of the important things. We were sent off to Drass in the evening itself.

At that time, our battalion was fighting on the Tololing mountain in the Drass sector. I was thrilled to be in the middle of action and prayed to god for the victory of our Army.

> *Destiny gives only a few the chance to fulfil long-cherished dreams. When the opportunity arises, embrace it with passion.*

28

The Face-off at the Tololing Mountain

20 May 1999

Our battalion was fighting a fierce battle on the Tololing peak to keep up its own honour as well as the sovereignty of the country. The Tololing peak is strategically situated, adjacent to National Highway 1A. It was the only lifeline highway for Leh and Srinagar. The Pakistan army had extended its post up to the lower parts of the mountain which had blocked our national highway. All our supplies to Leh had been blocked completely as a result. The most crucial task for the Army was to capture the Tololing peak and unblock the road so as to restart sending supplies through that route.

The Commanding Officer of our Unit, Col. Khushal Chand Thakur[6] made a very good plan on the basis of his experience from previous operations.

Then he explained the war strategy to all the company commanders. This plan was based on the information from local persons, information available from the headquarters and his own knowledge and experiences about war. At that time, whatever information was available, pointed to the presence of terrorists on the peaks.

His experiences in this field, along with his planning and way of functioning, had been of great help to us in the Unit in the Kashmir valley, helping us to eliminate terrorists. On the basis of this war planning and strategy, the unit started climbing the Tololing mountain. We knew that the enemy was on the top; we would have to keep ourselves hidden from them in order to move forward.

The entire Unit, with its war cry 'Savrada Shaktishali'[7], set off to achieve its end. The soldiers marched on in their groups, shoulder to shoulder, fully charged and determined to win the war. They seemed to be somewhat like tigers that had tasted blood.

Our Unit had carried out Operation Jativad on mountains like these a few months ago. In the course of that operation, which had continued for seventy-two hours, many terrorists

---

6. Now Brig (Retd) Khushal Thakur, he is actively working for people's rights and welfare.
7. Literally, always powerful, it is the Grenadiers' motto.

had been caught and eliminated on the narrow and intricate mountain roads. But in those days, the mountains were full of trees which ensured that there was plenty of oxygen. At that height, since the oxygen is less, if there is greenery all around, it is easy to work and one does not have to carry oxygen cylinders.

The mountains of Tololing were just the opposite, absolutely stony. There was no greenery around us, therefore, no oxygen coming from them. And Drass was a place where the temperature goes down to -60 degrees Celsius in winter. In the month of May too, the temperature was close to -20 degrees Celsius. The soldiers of the unit depended on their training, experience and expert leadership to guide them on their mission.

On the first night after starting off for the peak, the Unit had neared the top. At that time, the enemy started firing. They were stunned to see us so close to them.

Every soldier knows that the first step of success is taking your enemy by surprise. If one suddenly sees that the enemy soldier is very close, half their courage is gone. For example, if you have secured your house fully and still someone breaks into it, you are at a complete loss. Even if you have weapons, you cannot use them promptly. This 'surprise element' was very helpful to us in this case as well.

On the battlefield, surprising the enemy and getting close to him shatters his morale and disrupts his planning. At the same time, it displays our meticulous planning and work skills. It was with this planning that Unit 2 reached the top of the mountain.

But even till this point, we did not have clarity that these were Pakistani soldiers on our posts, not terrorists.

Terrorists often have small weapons and hand grenades and our team had been equipped to fight against such groups. Since they continued firing at us with small weapons, there was no way to guess that these weren't terrorists but an army backed by bigger resources. Of course, we knew that the Pakistani army was supporting them, because at times, the firing was from artillery guns and mortar. From our end, one of the teams attacked the enemy on Tololing peak.

Subedar Lal Singh's team was the first to attack the enemy and his entire team was killed in action in the battle. We had been fighting with all our might for three days now, but had not been successful. The casualties were going up in our Unit, but success still seemed distant.

Our senior commanders kept constant watch on the situation. They were also upset at the high number of casualties and were trying to make an in-depth analysis of the entire situation. They were angry too; all of us were furious, to say the least. Col Thakur was under immense pressure, but no solution had been found so far. He had been bravely holding fort – devising the best strategies on the basis of the available information and also keeping the morale of the jawans high for the impending war.

On 26 May 1999, the Indian Air Force bombed those mountains so that the infantry could achieve its target. It was a two-pronged approach carried out with strategic planning. After all this, the situation should have come under control, but it remained the same.

On 28 May, the Commander of the B Company, Major Rajesh Adhikari was taken for an aerial survey of the area. When Major Adhikari surveyed the mountains, found out the real number of the terrorists and conducted a recce to find out their defensive positions, he was shocked. The number of terrorists which we had been told was around five was much more. It was close to twenty-five and they had made bunkers for themselves.

When he came back from the recce, he looked upset. I met him, as we had become friends. When we went for operations in Kashmir, I used to be with him. This was the same officer who had told me to take leave for one month instead of two as I would ask for leave to get married.

I knew there was something serious behind his frown that fateful day. Things were about to change drastically.

29

Major Rajesh Adhikari

When I had gone on leave for two months in January 1999, Major Adhikari had given me a letter and a few things to give to his family. They lived in Delhi and it fell on my way.

When I went to his house in Delhi, I met his parents and his wife Kiran ma'am. I gave them the things and the letter which Maj Adhikari had sent. They asked about him and this conversation went on for a long time. I answered them to the best of my ability from what all I had seen. I could understand that they were worried about sir.

Major Adhikari was very sociable and a music lover. He loved playing guitar. Whenever he came back from an operation, he would play his guitar and sing in order to relax. This pleased all the jawans in the company. When we went on search operations, he would sing while going there in the vehicle and on the way back. I was the most junior soldier in the Unit and he was quite senior. However, he and other seniors treated me like a friend and younger brother. I also loved him like an elder brother.

My other friend Yogendra and his comrade Hari sang together. All the members of the team also joined them when they sang. Adhikari sir usually joined in the singing. This is what transformed our *tukdi* into ten bodies with one soul.

I talked about all this to Adhikari sir's family, had tea with them and left for home.

♋

When I had asked him for leave for twenty days to get married, he had said, 'If you take leave now, you will not get any leave for seven months. Will you manage to be without leave for so long?'

I had said, 'Sir, I will have to. There is no choice.'

He had asked me, 'Have you met the girl? What does she do?'

I told him everything. 'Sir, my father has seen the girl in the village. He said that she is studying in the twelfth standard. I did not get a chance to see her. Dinesh sir's brother also got married in the same village, to her friend. But my mother did not let me go to the wedding.'

He had laughed a lot at this and said that my father would have made a wise choice for me.

I will always remember how he helped me at every step. His positive attitude and ringing laughter is etched in my memory.

♋

When I reached the Unit after coming back leave, Adhikari sir had come back after a recce of the mountains in a helicopter. As soon as he saw me, he said, 'So *dost*, you are back after your wedding. Why did you come back now, Yogendra? The situation is very bad. No one knows what will happen.'

I saw a strange kind of confusion mixed with sadness on his face and said, 'Sir, everything will be alright. Here, have some sweets that I have brought.'

He had some sweets and then I gave him some water. Then he started again, 'We are very close to the enemy,' he said that and went away.

This was our last meeting.

A and B Companies were deployed on the right side of the Tololong mountain and C and D companies on the left.

There was a team to provide ration and ammunition supplies to the A and B companies, but there was no such team for the C and D Companies. Fifteen jawans, including me, who had come back from leave, were ordered to supply ammunition and ration to these companies instead of being sent to their own companies.

I was very keen to go and fight on the front with my comrades, but it is a soldier's duty to obey orders. No soldier can disobey, because it is always part of a bigger plan about which he does not know. This is the sort of discipline which prevails in the Army.

Anyway, I suppressed my own desire of fighting at the front and became part of the team that supplied ammunition and ration. Whether it is war or something else, till all members of a team fulfil the task assigned to them, there can be no victory.

Later I realized that no task is small if we understand the significance of it.

I understood that it was because of our efforts that the jawans were fighting at the front. How would they fight if they did not get regular supplies of food and ammunition? They had full faith in us, that we would never let their supplies stop. We also trusted those jawans at the front that they would stop all bullets coming in our direction. There was complete faith in each other that neither would stop doing one's duty.

> *If you're going to live, leave a mark on the world that remains forever.*

30

Turning the Tide

On 28 May, When we were going towards the mountain, we noticed that three Indian Air Force helicopters were raining rockets and bullets atop the Tololing peak. When they were returning after having fired, the enemy suddenly attacked them with guided missiles. The Surface to Air Missile (SAM) struck the helicopter behind us and it caught fire immediately, falling in a canal on the other side of the mountain.

The pilots of that helicopter had managed to bail out with the help of a parachute, but they were captured by the enemy. They killed one and the other returned that very day. One Mig21 belonging to us was also shot down by the enemy in the Kargil sector. All these incidents made it clearer that these were no ordinary militants, but the Pakistan army holding the peak.

These extremely painful incidents shook up not only the Army, but the entire nation. It was now a question of the honour of the country. So, to teach the Pakistani army a lesson, a three-pronged operation started. The infantry started Operation Vijay, the Indian Air Force started Operation Safed Sagar and the Indian Navy started Operation Talwar – all three at the same time.

These three wings of the Indian Armed Forces are like the three points of lord Shiva's trishul, capable of achieving any aim, destroying any target in their united effort. They had resolved to keep up the honour of the tricolor and eliminate the enemy at any cost. They all jumped into the fray in full earnestness.

Our Air Force started raining bombs on the mountain peaks while the infantry fought with great courage on the ground. The Indian Navy surrounded the Karachi port.

That day, on 28 May, Major Rajesh Adhikari attacked the Tololing mountain with his team. They reached the bunkers of the enemy and there was fierce battle. All our soldiers were killed in action in this combat.

With this news, the unit went into deep anguish. Major Adhikari was a man par excellence and had won our hearts. His supreme sacrifice for the nation shook us till the roots, but we gathered ourselves and fought hard once again. Along with preserving the honour of our country, we also wanted to avenge for all our dear ones lost.

Before Major Adhikari's team had gone up, we had managed to collect the mortal remains of our fallen heroes and taken them to the base camp. But with Major Adhikari's team, the mortal remains were still lying in the bunkers of the enemy. A number of efforts were made to retrieve their bodies, but they were unsuccessful. The higher authorities were also raising questions now.

Senior commanders had a conversation with Col. Khushal Thakur. 'Col. Thakur, order your unit to climb down; we will send another platoon to do the work.'

But he was not to be browbeaten. True, we had not been able to capture the peaks yet, but he was sure of our victory. He said, 'Sir, this is the Unit from the Grenadiers Regiment. This same regiment had broken the morale of the Pakistani army completely in 1956. The Commanding Officer of the Unit does not only give commands, he is like a father to the entire Unit. All the soldiers are like his children. We will not leave without getting back the mortal remains of our children.'

All of us could understand the underlying emotion behind this, because we would never go anywhere, leaving our friends, our brothers behind. He said, 'Victory or death! Either my entire battalion will lay its life for the country and go down, or attain victory. No one will go down that mountain before that. Jai Hind!'

This increased the confidence of the senior officials. His powerful words inspired young jawans like us immensely. We started making plans about how to win Tololing and avenge the death of our comrades and get their mortal remains. It was a 'do or die' situation and we were ready to sacrifice our lives.

On 2 June 1999, an attack was launched under the leadership of Lt Col Ramakrishnan Vishwanathan, who was badly injured during the fight. He was brought to CO sir in that condition. He was still breathing but looked in bad shape. During that period, the jawan who was in charge of establishing communications, was also shot. When Col Thakur saw Vishwanathan sir in that condition, he felt helpless.

Thakur sir was trying to reassure him, but Vishwanathan sir kept on speaking – giving him crucial information about the situation on top of the Tololing mountain. He knew he would not live long, so he wanted to tell sir all that he had come to know and the position of the enemy, so that adequate planning could be done before the next attack, and casualties could be minimized. He continued to give all this information, though he could hardly breathe.

Col Thakur had also sensed that he did not have much time. While taking down all the information, he rang up his home through the satellite phone. His wife said, 'Hello' and at that very moment, Vishwanathan sir breathed his last. This was the biggest loss to our Unit as well as the Indian Army as he was a knowledgeable, conscientious, skilled and experienced officer. His intellectual skills were of the highest order. From the time he had become an officer, he used his skills in the field of training. He was invited to high level conferences because of these very skills. It pains us to have lost a jewel like him, but there is pride that he laid his life for the nation. He was posthumously awarded the Vir Chakra for his bravery and dedication to the nation.

> *We sleep safely at night because a soldier is awake, ensuring that the nation is in safe hands.*

31

Lt. Col. R. Vishwanathan

I remember, once when the CO had been on leave, Lt. Col. Vishwanathan was officiating in his place. As soon as he was in command, he launched an operation in Sumbal village in which the Unit had the opportunity to eliminate terrorists for the first time in eight months. But two of our jawans were also killed in this operation.

An announcement was made from the mosque in the village, early in the morning, for terrorists hidden in the village to come out of their houses. Two terrorists were hiding in the house right next to the mosque. As soon as they heard the announcement, they started firing at our team. It was being led by Vishwanathan sir. He sent a message to the rear that if anyone had a rocket launcher, he should come to the front. That particular day, I was one of the jawans who had come with the rocket launcher. That was also because our Company Havaldar Major had made me carry it as a punishment.

The previous night, our team had gone to a place where there had been some firing. When our team had gone to assist the team already there, we had to walk through the fields. As a result, my shoes were full of mud. By the time we reached the team, the terrorists had fled to the mountains.

We returned at about 2 a.m. The next morning, we were supposed to meet the 2IC. During such a meeting, a soldier has to maintain a certain decorum regarding his dress. My uniform was in order, but my shoes were not shining. I had washed them the previous night and since they did not dry, no matter how much polish I put on them, they wouldn't shine. The Company Havaldar Major was in charge of the discipline, he said to me angrily, 'Give them to me, I will make them shine!'

As soon as the meeting was over, orders came from the unit headquarter that we would have to go on foot to Sumbal village where an operation was scheduled. As soon as the order came, the CHM called me and ordered, 'You will carry the rocket launcher.'

I said, 'Sir, I don't know how to use it.'

He said, 'The leader of the team is there to use it. You have to carry it.'

I agreed and took it up. Now that weapon weighs sixteen kilos; there are rockets weighing four kilos each. Along with all that, I had to carry my AK-47 rifle and ammunition, altogether around 25-30 kilos. Anyway, I marched on foot with the rocket launcher as ordered.

When Vishwanathan sir asked for it, my team leader told me to take it to him. We had taken position near the houses on the outskirt of the village and were sitting there. The main road of the village was in front of us, and the terrorists were firing constantly. Then I reached there with the weapon.

Vishwanathan sir said, 'Beta, do you know how to fire it?'

I said, 'No sir, I don't know. I joined the Unit only nine months back.'

He said very affectionately, 'It's okay.'

After that, he himself fired it, got out from there and organized a search operation team.

Major Rajesh Adhikari's team searched the village for two days. In that operation, one terrorist was killed.

I had the opportunity to work with him from June to August 1998, looking after the safety of the Amarnath pilgrims.

Vishwanathan sir was an upright and efficient officer. His death sent the whole Unit into a state of shock. The blood of every jawan boiled to avenge his death. On top of that, the pressure now was to come down the mountain if we couldn't win, and let some other unit take over. There was a lot of chaos as time was of the essence. In the face of all this pressure, our CO was determined. He repeated, 'We will come down only after attaining victory, or else you can get our bodies.' Then he added, 'If you want to help us, send us re-enforcement.'

At this request, teams from 2 Rajputana Rifles were deployed to re-enforce us as well as take part in the attacks.

The CO of Rajputana Rifles, Col. Ravindra had a meeting with the higher authorities, where ground realities were discussed. Our forces needed a lot of artillery support to win.

The enemy could not be beaten only by small weapon attacks. How could foot soldiers get near them and defeat them?

After a lot of discussion, artillery guns were also deployed in the Kargil-Batalik sector.

But the artillery guns were not supposed to be fired near the Line of Control (LoC). This war was also to show the world the moral and immoral aspect of fighting. Their artillery guns were firing blindly at our Army as well as civil areas, whereas our guns fired only at those posts within the LoC which the enemy had captured.

After 4-5 June 1999, the jawans of 2 Rajputana Rifles also carried their ammunition up the mountain. Our teams were taking regular supplies of ammunition and rations. It was the night of 9 or 10 June when we were going up to take supplies of ammunition and rations for our comrades. The team of Rajputana Rifles was also with us. We had to sit and rest after every ten steps because of the low level of oxygen. We were sitting under a big stone and the jawans from Rajputana Rifles were also there.

There were seven soldiers from the same family, some were Subedar, Havaldar and others. One of them was saying, 'Sir, we are from the same family. You don't need to get seven coffins, you can send our mortal remains in the same coffin.'

From their words, it seemed to me that the soldier of the Indian Army thinks of the welfare of his country even after he has drawn his last breath.

Tough times become easier to fight when we look out for each other and keep the spirits high, come what may!

32

The Tricolor on the Tololing Peaks

Finally, on 12 June, plans were made to launch an attack on the Tololing mountain. I remember, from the evening itself, our artillery guns started firing towards the top of Tololing mountain. Hundreds of guns were firing at the same time. As the cannonballs hit the mountain and burst, the shrapnel scattered far and wide and set fire to everything they struck.

We climbed the mountain throughout the night and could see all this. In the morning, when the Rajputana Rifles attacked, many of our enemies had been killed by the canon fire. Only a few of them had survived.

During the attack, officers of the Rajputana Rifles and quite a few soldiers laid their lives. However, this was the first successful encounter of the Indian Army, despite the heavy price that had to be paid for winning back the Tololing mountain.

This first victory boosted the morale of the Army. At the same time, the confidence of the Pakistani army had gone down considerably. Unit 2 of the Rajputana Rifles had come down after this victory. It was not a personal victory for our Unit and we were ordered to attack the 7 other peaks on the Tololing mountain, to capture them and avenge the death of our comrades.

We were planning the attack on 23 June. The morale of our jawans was very high. One victory had changed the whole scene and soldiers in all sectors were determined to keep it up. They were geared up for that with all their heart.

We were being briefed for the attack. In the enthusiasm of it, a Pakistani artillery gun fired at us and many of our jawans were killed, with their limbs scattered all over in splashes of blood. Here, we had been standing listening to the instructions, and in one moment, the scene changed. We had not dreamt of such a great tragedy right before the attack. An air of gloom prevailed over the whole unit, but the burning rage to avenge these deaths was equally strong.

Many jawans were deployed to take the dead bodies down and the rest attacked the peaks with full gusto. In this way, on 24 June 1999, we captured all seven peaks by morning and avenged the deaths of our comrades. The national tricolor once again flew on all the peaks of the Tololing mountain.

After the success of the Unit on the Tololing peaks, we were ordered to climb down. We took all our weapons and ammunition and started the climb downwards. Our place was taken by 13 Jammu and Kashmir Rifles. We saw to it that they were stationed at the posts we had captured. It took us two or three days to reach the base camp along with all our ammunition and weapons.

Once we had reached the base camp, the realization struck. We knew that many of our comrades had given the supreme sacrifice. The rest of us could hardly recognize each other – everyone had long overgrown beards. The faces had become black and the skin appeared cracked as no one had taken a bath for almost a month now. None of us had eaten properly so we had lost a lot of weight. We had been on duty day and night.

After about one month, we bathed and started to look after our weapons and other belongings, after checking the state they were in. Then we waited for our next task. We had the feeling that we had learnt a lot from these mountains. When the next deployment came, we started once again with renewed vigour, to avenge the death of our comrades and win glory for our beloved nation.

Victory comes to those who march on towards their goal, undeterred by any challenge that comes their way.

33

The War on Tiger Hill

We were waiting at Matiyan for our next transfer when all of a sudden, the CO called a general assembly of all the soldiers. He informed us about our next task.

We had been assigned a significant and challenging task of avenging the deaths of our fellow soldiers by recapturing an important post. We had to attain victory by recapturing Tiger Hill.

The area of Tiger Hill had earlier been given to another Brigade. But this task was assigned to us keeping in view our strategic planning as well as courageous performance on the Tololing mountain. So, to keep up the reputation of our regiment 18 Grenadiers, we were expected to be victorious in this task as well.

In this assembly, the CO gave all the relevant information about the task for the company teams to all the jawans present. He explained everything – how to launch attacks on Tiger Hill and the order in which each company and team was to proceed during the attack. The assembly lasted for about an hour and the jawans were told where each battalion was to be deployed.

It is true that when jawans are told about their tasks in detail – along with strategies regarding the forthcoming war action – they are able to give their own suggestions in the matter as per their experience and intelligence. These suggestions could make the plan work even better. If the planning is good, members of the team can cope with the most challenging situations and prepare themselves mentally to be able to face all kinds of difficulties.

Everyone knows clearly what the task before him is. Since the plan has suggestions from everyone by way of inputs, it is sure to succeed and result in victory. Also, the experiences of the battle of Tololing were still fresh in our minds. On the basis of that experience and elaborate planning among soldiers, we were able to work out a detailed war strategy with regard to Tiger Hill.

Tiger Hill was the highest peak in the Drass sector. The enemy was stationed and keeping an eye on the entire Drass sector from the top. He could track each and every movement made by us and also knew that we had captured the lower peaks and mountains in that sector. Taking advantage of the height of its position, the enemy constantly bombed us, increasing the number of casualties on our side.

It was very important to capture those heights in order to put a stop to our casualties. In a mountainous area, it is important to capture the highest peak in order to establish one's supremacy in the area, because from a position at the top, you can control the whole situation as well as examine the movements of the enemy.

At this point of time, the Pakistani army had captured all the high peaks and was stationed there, keeping a close watch on our Army, apart from provocative firing.

Very serious discussions were carried out and it was decided that the high peaks in all sectors should be captured so that the enemy could be eliminated in the true sense of the word.

Our Army was capturing the multiple lesser altitude peaks and killing the enemy, or pushing them back. But the final decision was that high peaks should be attacked and captured for supremacy in the area.

It was not at all easy to capture these high peaks, but the Indian Army is known for making impossible tasks possible. Keeping up the same tradition, Tiger Hill in the Drass sector had to be captured.

As soon as our unit was given this task, the jawans got busy with the preparations to do it honourably and bring glory to the regiment, Army and the country. Another Unit was deployed by the base camp in order to help ours.

In accordance with the planning of the unit commander, the attacking platoon would attack the enemy from the back on Tiger Hill. C and D Companies would help the attacking platoon in this. A Company would attack the enemy from the front. B Company was kept in reserve, to be sent for help wherever needed.

In this way, after the planning was completed, jawans were chosen from all four companies for initiating the attack. Those who had been found physically and mentally fit even after the fighting on Tololing mountain were given priority. Because the height of this mountain was 16,500 ft, there was a great shortage of oxygen. So both experienced and new jawans were included in the team.

Our team had been an attacking one from the beginning. But a number of members of this team had been lost in the fighting on the Tololing mountain, and their places had to be filled.

At this point, I want to tell you that in a battle, a person is known not by his rank, but by his actions and presence of mind in the battlefield. At that time, I was known as the number one Rifleman of Section 1 of the B team. This was my only identity. I had not been born with special powers, nor had I been selected in the Army for any special skills. I had been selected through a regular process.

I was an ordinary soldier like everyone else when I fought in the Tololing battle.

When I had reported back after my leave, our team of jawans was fighting bravely. We were given the task of reinforcing them with ammunition and other things that they needed. In the team, there were three, including me, who did their duty for twenty-two days, without resting or sleeping.

We would start from the base camp at 5 in the morning and reach at around 2.30 in the night. We would have to climb up and down in the midst of heavy artillery firing from the enemy.

My way of looking at my work earlier was responsible for getting selected as part of the attacking platoon. My desire to fight the enemy was also fulfilled. I considered myself lucky to be selected as part of the team.

♋

The team selected for this operation was significant as the responsibility of upholding the reputation of the entire Unit depended on it. At that time, a new officer had been commissioned to our unit. He was appointed as the commander of this platoon. His name was Lt. Balwan Singh. We were very happy with his leadership. He gave us all the support we needed, always walking by our side.

We started planning for the completion of our task and embarked upon the toughest of exercises. We practiced very hard, going through the most gruelling regime, removing our weak points and taking care of the smallest things that mattered. When we practice, we gain confidence in our own equipments, weapons, the leader as well as ourselves. This faith in oneself and devotion to work is the surest way to attain success.

Finally after our own preparations and the planning of our senior officials, it was decided that we should attack on 2 July 1999.

That day finally came.

I firmly believe that the whole world is based on faith. The Indian Army does not believe in any one religion or culture; it is an organization which respects all religions and cultures. People conduct a havan or puja before embarking on some auspicious work. Our Battalion Commander also arranged a havan to pray for the success of the operation and to boost the morale of the unit in general. The havan was in memory of the comrades who had sacrificed their lives. It was also for us to sacrifice all our fears of death in the holy fire. After the havan, we started making preparations to start that very evening.

> *I have always regarded this life as an ocean and churning pot of actions. One's feelings are like the rope in the churning pot, which helps one in the process of churning. It is the same in our lives too. It is your way of thinking which determines the results that you get from your actions.*

34

Ready for Action

We got our weapons and other things ready by the afternoon. We were sleeping in two tents to energize ourselves. We all knew how delicate the times to come would be, maybe we would not even get time to write a letter after this day. So all of us sat during the time of our rest and started writing letters home. I wrote two letters, one for my newly wedded wife and the other one for my parents. It was difficult for me to write these letters, but it was my duty and I was determined to do it.

After writing the letters, we slept for a short while. It is said that if something bad is about to happen, one gets an indication of it beforehand. It is another thing that we often ignore such signs. We are generally ruled by our mind and do what it tells us to do. But we forget that our soul is a part of the almighty. It informs the individual from time to time as to what is going to happen. But we fail to understand these signs and blame god for anything bad that happens to us. Why blame god! He had already forewarned us about what was going to happen. If man does not understand the messages sent by god, I personally feel it is his fault.

During my stay in the camp, I felt that man is always vested with godly power. I experienced this when we slept for a short time after writing the letters.

While I was sleeping, I dreamt that I had been hit by a number of bullets and was bleeding profusely. My whole body was bloody. At this point, I woke up and there was such a severe storm that our entire tent was uprooted and blown to the foot of the mountain. Some jawans ran to catch hold of the tent, others were busy in collecting our things which were now scattered due to the piercing wind.

The letters written by us also flew away in the storm. Someone told me to find the letters. I tried very hard, but could find only one letter written by each of us, whereas we had written more. Then we gave all the letters that had been retrieved to a JCO so that he could post them the next day. We collected all our belongings and kept the ones that we were taking with us on one side.

In the evening, we were sent close to Tiger Hill in an Army vehicle. After travelling for close to two hours, we reached the village near the foothills. We had something to eat and waited for darkness to fall. This was to avoid being seen by the enemy which was at a height and thus, an advantageous point. If we were seen climbing, we would be finished even before we reached them.

That was why we were supposed to keep all our movements secret from the enemy. We wanted to reach their posts without being detected.

When it became very dark, we were ordered to start climbing Tiger Hill. As soon as the order came, our team started the steep climb. The level of oxygen was very low because of the high altitude and each jawan was carrying about 25 to 30 kilos of weight on his back.

The wind was icy cold and the climb was steep. The load on our backs was heavy and to top it all, there was very little oxygen. However, we carried on without caring. The climb was very difficult. We were getting breathless after every fifty steps. Then we would sit and rest for a short while and start again. In this way, we covered some of the distance in the course of the night. We reached the spot where 8 Sikh Battalion had set up a firm base. A firm base is a secure place from where we could attack the enemy, but it was impossible for the enemy to attack us. By the time we reached the firm base, it was morning.

We had been told to hide ourselves behind the big rocks during daylight. We spent the entire day without eating or drinking anything, not even doing things that are part of our daily routine. When it became dark again, we knew that we would soon get the order to move again. So we made some tea on the stoves that we had brought. We had some biscuits and *shakkarparas*[8] and started climbing again.

Climbing forward was getting more and more difficult. As we reached a higher altitude, there was less and less oxygen, but

---

8. A sweet snack.

the icy winds were getting tougher to handle. We did not stop despite all these challenges. What guided us along was the faith and trust that our country had put in us. It was very essential for us to keep it intact. It was this faith and our relentless conviction that made us go on the whole night.

> *Sometimes our will becomes our biggest inspiration. When there is no force helping us in our task, we must look inwards to get the desired strength.*

35

The Steep Climb to the Top

By the next morning, we reached the foothill of a peak. In a mountainous area, when we look at a mountain from a distance, we see only its main peak. But as we approach closer, the main peak disappears from view. We had the same experience.

When we reached close to the mountain, we did not see the main peak, but only the first peak. We were under the mistaken belief that it was the Tiger Hill top.

Along with us, another Company was also moving as a support team. Captain Sachin Nimbalkar[9] was the Commanding Officer of the Delta company. He told the leader of our team, 'Balwan, this seems to be Tiger Hill. Let us set up our camp here.'

9. He was awarded the prestigious Vir Chakra for his exploits in the battlefield.

As we climbed that peak, we saw another peak. That's when we realized that the peak in the distance was Tiger Hill, not the one we had just reached. Then we started moving towards that peak.

We kept on climbing, hiding ourselves from view. Strangely enough, when we reached that peak, we saw another peak ahead of us. We had been climbing the whole day and night without food and water. We were so tired that we found it difficult to breathe. We started the deployment of our arms on that peak.

One of our teams was sent to recce whether there were any soldiers of the enemy close by. At that point of time, we were so exhausted that if the enemy was around and got to know of our position, we would not even have the strength to use our weapons against them. So in order to protect ourselves from them, we thought it was wise to search the area carefully.

When our soldiers were visible from the top, searching near the peak, the enemy fired at them. B Team was in front of us. They shouted from where they were, 'Get us out of here!'

We could not even fire from the front as that would put our own soldiers in the line of fire. It was the same thing with firing the artillery guns. We called out to them to remain behind the rocks. We would take them out when it became dark.

At around 11 that night, we managed to bring them to safety. One of the soldiers was shot in the arm, while all others were unhurt. The soldier who had been injured was crying out in pain. It was a mix of pain, shock and a sense of helplessness, I presumed. This was the second jawan I had seen crying after being hit. I thought that it must hurt a lot if one got shot.

He was sent down that night. At once, there was a command from the Battalion commander that an attack should be mounted at once. We started preparing ourselves for the attack at about midnight. We left our heavy belongings there and started talking among ourselves.

One said, 'If I die, give half of my money to my wife and the other half to my parents.'

My senior Yogendra and I were in that team. He also said to me, 'If I die, give half my money to my wife so that she can take care of our daughter, and the other half to my parents.'

I told him the same thing, though I was just newly married. Then I wondered aloud, 'What if both of us die? Who would tell our families what to do!' I could not think anymore.

I said, 'Let's write all this down in the notebook that I have.'

He agreed and we got down to it.

In that notebook, we wrote all that we had to say and kept it in my backpack. This thought had come to us because we knew that the enemy was not far from us. They were placed in a stronger position in comparison. The climb to the tallest peak that started from there was very tough. We would either be able to conquer the peak and place our tricolor there; or come back wrapped in the country's flag. There was no other option.

Just after we had finished writing in our notebook, the command came for us to start climbing. Yogendra and I were asked to lead the team. We were fully capable of fulfilling our duties. Our own safety, along with our team's, was now our responsibility.

I was walking slowly with my team, carefully scanning the entire area. The enemy could be anywhere. Who knew which rock could turn out to be the last one we crossed, or where the enemy sat, ready to pounce upon us. So we treaded carefully at every step.

We had not gone far when we started getting out of breath. The lack of oxygen at this altitude was crippling for the best of us. So we moved bit by bit, resting every now and then to catch our breath and stabilize our bodies.

In a few minutes, we came upon a cliff which seemed impossible to climb. It was imperative for us to go to the other side if we wished to reach Tiger Hill. We threw a rope up and it got stuck somewhere. Then we climbed up the cliff, uphill along the steep climb, with the help of that rope. I was the first to pull myself on top of the cliff. Once I was there, I looked around, ensuring a clear ground around me. I carefully tied the rope to a rock. Then the other jawans climbed up, helping each other.

The little sounds made by our feet touching the rock and dislodging a few small stones in the process were rather loud in the deathly silent night. As the stones fell, they also made a sound. At night, when it is quiet all around, even a low sound seems like a piercing one.

I noticed that the sky had started getting lighter. Perhaps, it was close to dawn. All of a sudden, the soldiers from the Pakistani bunkers on both sides of the cliff started firing at us. By that time, just about seven of us had managed to climb up. The rest were curtailed due to the heavy firing from both the sides.

Our route was now cut off. The rest of the party was unable to climb up and those of us who were up there already, were unable to go either left or right. The seven of us climbed up further ahead and saw a large plain area. There were two bunkers right in front of us. We took positions and started firing. Within moments, we had managed to kill the Pakistani soldiers in those bunkers in direct, face to face firing. We could finally see the Tiger Hill ahead of us.

That plain was the enemy's point of defense. In our quick recce of the area, we could estimate about a hundred and fifty Pakistani soldiers stationed around us. When they heard the sound of our firing, they also started firing on us very heavily, from all sides.

Indian soldiers are not taught to step back, and in the given scenario, moving forward meant sure death. We were surrounded on all sides. In a situation, when death seems to be the only option, fear vanishes. After all, we were soldiers who had been living in the midst of heavy firing for quite some time now. I was not afraid of death. All I prayed for was to not die before winning back Tiger Hill.

Do you know what empowers the Indian soldier the most? It is his mindset and the readiness to sacrifice for his country. His body could be full of bullets, but till the last drop of blood in his body, he marches on to eliminate the enemy.

When a soldier sacrifices himself for the nation, his locality, village and the whole country mourns. The marks of bullets on his chests adorn him like ornaments. This is what empowers the Army and the whole country.

Trapped in that situation, I thought to myself that we would die if we had to, but before that, we must defeat our enemy.

With this thought in mind, we rushed towards the enemy bunkers. We threw out the dead bodies of the Pakistani soldiers and took over the bunkers. Then, fierce fighting started. There was heavy firing from both the sides. They constantly fired their artillery guns and their mortars. But we responded to their fire with patience and courage.

This went on for five long hours. It must have been around 11:00 a.m. The Indian soldiers were determined to win and no one could deter them from their purpose or move them from what they had already captured.

After fighting the enemy for such a long time, our ammunition was running out. We called out to our comrades below to send us fresh supplies. They did send us some ammunition tied in handkerchiefs, but we could not move even a single step this side or that side, being surrounded by the enemy.

Their bullets flew from over our heads. If we moved even a little or raised our heads, we could be hit by their bullets. So we were not even able to pick up the ammunition thrown up by our team below. Then we planned to kill the Pakistani soldiers close to us, hiding behind the rocks, so that we could use their ammunition.

We decided not to fire back at the Pakistani soldiers for a while. They were sure to come out from behind the rocks when we stopped firing to check if we were dead. We could take advantage of that. With this resolution, we took our positions behind rocks and hid ourselves well. The Pakistani soldiers fired at us for some time, but stopped when they did not hear any firing in response. There was a deadly silence on our side.

They kept watching the situation for minutes, wondering why we were not firing or making any sound. Finally, after waiting and watching for a long time, they emerged from behind the huge boulders. We were absolutely calm, watching them, almost holding our breath to not make a sound.

We saw that there was a very big rock in front of us. One by one, they were emerging from behind it. When they all stood there, right in front of us, all of us fired at them together. Except for one or two, all of them were killed instantly.

Taking advantage of the situation, we ran from behind the rocks to where their bodies lay and took away their weapons and ammunition. Then we took position behind the rocks again. We knew that now we would be attacked by a large group of soldiers. They would launch a big attack on us to avenge the death of their fellows.

We started making plans to foil that attack and defeat them.

We tried to make our position safe and secure from the firing of the enemy. We wanted to be in an attacking position as well. We had just started to implement our plan when heavy firing started again. Our work of securing the bunkers was left incomplete. We silently waited for them to come close to us.

I remember that while heavy firing was going on, we were not even in a condition to lift ourselves up. After firing for quite some time, the Pakistani soldiers stopped, thinking they had won. They cried, 'Allahu Akbar' and started throwing stones at us. Such big stones being thrown from the top of the mountain can be more lethal than bullets. Some were throwing grenades as well. We remained patient and calm, waiting for them to come close. We could sense from the sound of their footsteps that they were approaching us slowly. Since there was no sound on our side, they were coming closer fearlessly.

We had hidden ourselves in spaces between the rocks and were watching their movement closely. We wanted them to come in front of us so that they were totally exposed and had no place to hide. Then, we could kill them. The timing of the fire would be crucial if we wanted to kill them all in one go. We fully realized that this was a real battlefield and there was no scope of error. Of course it was easier said than done. It was obvious that they would fire three times more than us as they were more in number.

Somewhere, we knew this could be our last few minutes, but we wanted to kill the maximum number of Pakistani soldiers before our breath left our bodies.

Suddenly, a grenade hit the light machine gun (LMG) on my right. Our heavy weapons were totally destroyed. Those deployed to fire the gun were hit by stones on the head and chest and they ran to Havaldar Madan, asking for help.

Immediately, Platoon Commander Havaldar Madan said to me, 'Yogendra, pick up that LMG and throw it to me. I can fix the spare barrel on to it and make it fit for firing.'

I threw it to him at once. That was the last time I heard my Platoon Commander's voice.

Now they knew about our movement and position. So they rained grenades and bullets on us. One grenade burst right next to me at the back, and my comrade Yogendra's finger was severed by it. We gave him first aid, while still being bombarded from both sides.

It went on like this for a very long time. Every moment, some or the other comrade was getting hurt or breathing his last. But we had made up our minds – we would not retreat, come what may!

I noticed that a fellow who fired sniper rifles, was surrounded by Pakistanis. So Anant Ram, a comrade who had trained with me, and I had to go to him to help. As soon as I advanced towards him to help, a grenade fell near me and burst. A shrapnel from it hit me behind my knee. The piercing pain made me feel like my leg had been cut off.

As I fell, I looked back to see the extent of damage the grenade had done. I noticed that the leg had not been cut off, but the wound was very deep. I started giving myself first aid. As I was doing it, another grenade burst in front of me and a shrapnel hit me under my eye and nose, causing a deep wound. I felt that I had lost my eyes.

For a long time, I could see nothing. I lay there behind the rock. With time, I could see some light seeping into my eyes. When I looked at myself, I saw that my whole body was covered with blood. My nose was bleeding heavily. I tried hard to control it, but in vain. Then I mustered up all my courage and somehow dragged myself to my comrade Lance Naik Naresh Kumar. He was trying to make his bunker higher and firing back at those who were firing at him, all at the same time.

I sat with my back to a rock and started firing, trying to clean the blood from my nose. Then I told Naresh to give me first aid as I had lost a lot of blood. He looked at me and said, 'I'll do it soon. Keep on firing.'

I said, 'Right sir.'

After some time, he took his field *patti* from his pocket. Just as he raised his hand to open it, a bullet hit him on the head. His head burst open and blood oozed out.

I held his hand because he was falling backwards. I could still only see hazily, so I wasn't sure what had happened.

I said, 'What happened sir? Say something!'

I couldn't hear anything except gunfire, and I understood what must have happened.

Anant Ram was sitting by my side. I said to him, 'Sir has been hit by a bullet.'

He was stunned. Just as he was about to say something, a bullet hit him on the chest and he was gone in a moment.

I called out to my mates down below, 'Sir, two jawans have been hit.'

A voice asked, 'How are they?'

I tried to sound brave as I said, 'We have lost them, sir.'

I could say only this when bullets rained on us afresh. The enemy had surrounded us on three sides.

That was indeed a very painful moment. Even today when I start talking about it, when I think about the brave and dutiful soldiers who laid down their lives for their country, tears start flowing from my eyes.

There were three or four of us and the enemies were no less than thirty-five. The guns spewed fire and bodies of soldiers of both sides lay scattered. The last thought of our jawans was that their own deaths did not matter; the Army should win.

All my comrades had laid down their lives for their country. I was partially sitting among them, my body covered with blood. I remembered the lines I had heard somewhere.

Boundaries are not drawn on paper in ink; they are made up by the swords of the brave.

The enemy shot at my fellows, who were already dead, to ensure that they weren't alive.

Today, I was seeing for myself how we had sacrificed every inch of our bodies in killing the enemy. Now the boundary of the country was indicated by the blood of our bravehearts who had laid down their lives, defending the motherland. I had resolved not to leave the battlefield till there was even one drop of blood in my body.

A soldier takes on the work of his comrades who have been killed in action. I took on the resolve of my comrades on myself and prayed to god to give me strength to complete the work which they could not.

If you pray to god sincerely and selflessly, he helps you with his own incredible powers. I lay absorbed in my thoughts, watching what the Pakistani soldiers were up to. A few Pakistani soldiers shot at the dead, and the bodies jumped with the impact of bullets. As I was watching all this, a Pakistani soldier started firing at me. He shot at my left hand and right leg. I could see a sort of smoke coming out of the places where the bullets hit me.

I lay quietly in spite of the intolerable pain. No soldier leaves his enemy alive. These soldiers were firing at us to see if anyone was alive. Finally, they were convinced that everyone on our side had died.

I lay helpless, suppressing my pain, but did not lose my mental strength. My spirituality helped me maintain calm in the face of such grave adversity. I kept up my courage and patience. In a situation like this, it is very important to be in full control of your senses. I was looking for an opportunity when they became careless and I could do something.

Just then, their commander sent a message to their base camp in Mushkoh valley. He said, 'We have killed a group of Hindustani soldiers who had come near the top. There is a medium machine gun post below. You wait for us there. We are coming down.'

I heard this. I thought if they are able to go down, my entire team would be wiped out. Unable to think of a way to stop them, I prayed to god, 'Oh almighty, give me enough strength so that I am able to send this information to my mates to save their lives.'

Just then, their commander said, 'Take possession of their weapons.'

One Pakistani soldier was shooting at the dead bodies, the other one was picking up the weapons lying near the bodies. He again shot at my arms and legs and I bore the pain. The bones and flesh were sticking out of my arms and legs. I did not care about that. I told myself that I would not die unless they shot me on the head or chest. I would not let out the slightest groan even if they cut off both my arms and legs. I think this mental strength came in handy and I held fort with some spiritual energy.

I had let this thought fill my mind – I *will not die unless I am hit on the head or chest.*

It is true that if you let any thought sink firmly into your mind and subconscious, your hormones act accordingly. Our body also responds accordingly to our hormones. I had convinced myself that I would not die unless shot on the chest or the head. Just then, the Pakistani soldier turned back and pointed his gun at my chest.

I was watching all this with eyes half closed. It is said that if you surrender yourself selflessly, god protects you by taking you within himself. I had surrendered fully to god. In that moment, I realized why we referred to our country as Mother India. The land on which I lay was not just sand, stones and pebbles; it was a living being. This mother has never let the courage and bravery of her sons go waste. That day too, she saved me.

Perhaps, at that moment, she decided to listen to my plea. The soldier did shoot at me, but the bullet hit the coins in a wallet in my pocket and was deflected in another direction.

When the bullet hit me, I thought I had died. But no one can kill you if god does not will it. Then another Pakistani soldier came close to me. He took my AK 47 and walked away. I think his foot touched my leg, and the shooting pain suddenly left a burst of consciousness. I realized that I was alive.

Then a voice within me said, 'You are alive. Nobody can kill you now. I took out a grenade, removed its pin and threw it at the Pakistani soldier. It got stuck in his jacket's hoodie and he looked back. But he saw only what he thought were dead bodies. He did not realize that the grenade was still stuck in his hoodie. He tried to take it off his jacket.

In the meantime, the grenade burst.

Half of his head disappeared and he fell on us. The explosion startled the Pakistanis who had started celebrating their victory, thinking they were quite safe now. It caused a grave chaos among them.

Some said that they should fire in this direction; others said it was no use as we were all dead. They should fire in the other direction. Some felt that another team of Indian soldiers must have come up.

As they were confused regarding what course of action to take, I pushed away the dead body of the Pakistani soldier on top of me and extended both my hands to grab his rifle. I realized then that my right shoulder was moving, but the rest of the arm was numb.

I picked up the rifle with one hand and fired from behind the rock. Four soldiers of the enemy were killed in this firing. Then I fired again from behind another rock. In this way, I changed location and fired from three to four different locations. They felt that the Indian forces had come up from below and attacked them from different points behind the rocks.

This renewed attack devastated them completely. They started running towards the top. I also dragged myself from behind the rocks and kept on firing at them. When I noticed how they were running away to save their lives, I understood the difference between the enemy soldiers and us.

I chased them for about five metres by dragging my lifeless body. I looked down and noticed that their langar was in progress. I could see where their deployment of weapons and their living tents were. I watched all this for quite some time and saved it all in my memory. I kept on thinking of ways to save our post and fellow soldiers. After stopping there for some time, I dragged myself to where my fellow soldiers were. Slowly, I crawled to where my comrades lay.

I wondered if one of them might be alive, like me. I could hear someone breathing. I looked at them – One had his head blown apart and the bullets had ripped open the chest and body of another. Looking for someone who was still bodies in that pile of dead bodies was like looking for water in a desert. I felt very disappointed and wept a lot. Then I tried to console myself and pepped up myself to do something.

The broken bone of my left arm had come out of the body. It seemed as if the arm had been cut off from below the shoulder. When the shoulder bone rubbed against the cut off pieces of bone on the arm, the pain was intolerable. I bore the pain as best as I could, but I knew I had to do something fast.

I constantly prayed to god to give me strength so that I could somehow go to the post below. When I looked around, I could see only mountains and snow. There seemed to be no way to get out of this place. I wondered what I could do at those critical circumstances.

On the other hand, my broken arm which was dangling started paining more and more. I had to do something. I had joined the Army at the tender age of seventeen and had served for two-and-a-half years. I was barely nineteen now so I had no experience to deal with such a situation. My only aim was to fulfill what I wanted to do. If I had any power of speech left, the last words would be '*Vande Mataram*'.

With this feeling, I tried to keep the broken part of my arm away from my body so that it would hurt less. If man tries to work selflessly even in his last hours, he is helped by divine powers. It was as if someone was telling me, 'Go down this way!'

I tucked my dangling arm in my belt so that it didn't interfere with my movement. Then, I started rolling down in the direction my heart pointed at. Finally, I managed to roll down in a *nallah* below.

I could see a deep abyss below me and I hung there, clinging on to a rock. I started wondering if I had come to the Pakistani side. As I looked below me to my left and right, I could see some soldiers. Fortunately, I recognized one of them. He had been with us, but was unable to come up because of the firing. I called out to him for help. He looked up and could see a soldier hanging on to a rock. Immediately, two or three soldiers came to me and got me down from the rock.

When they looked at my condition, they thought I was going to die. Of course, they gave me false assurances that nothing had happened to me and I would soon be alright.

I said more confidently than ever, 'Nothing will happen to me. Those soldiers are going to attack this post. Save it.'

Those soldiers did my dressing. I told them everything that had happened up there. When our CO Col. Khushal Thakur was informed about me, he wanted to meet me immediately.

It must have been about 2:00 p.m. Since I had asked for water, some of my comrades went to fetch it. They had made me lie in the shade of a rock close to the nallah. A jawan who was sitting close to me was a friend and was constantly crying. I was drifting in and out of consciousness. I asked him, 'Sir, why are you crying?'

He said, 'Looking at you is making me cry.'

I said, 'Nothing will happen to me. Just give me some water. Why is it taking so long to get water?'

I did not know when they would be able to take me down. It is easy to climb up a mountain but tougher to go down, that too with a wounded soldier.

The soldiers came back after some time. They had also been hungry for two days. Maybe they had eaten something down there. After all, they would have to carry me down and then come up again.

They gave me some hot water to drink, then carried me down on their shoulders. I was carried to the CO. There, I was made to lie on a sleeping bag on a stretcher.

Immediately, CO Col. Thakur asked me, 'How are you, son?'

I said, 'I am fine sir. We lost all the soldiers up there. I am feeling very cold and cannot see anything.'

Hearing this, the CO made me lie in his tent where he lit three stoves. When the tent became warmer, I also felt warm.

Then he asked, 'Can you tell me what the situation is up there?'

I said, 'Of course sir. I can tell you everything.'

Then I described everything that had happened and he listened very carefully.

Then he asked me about our food rations. I said, 'Since we left you sir, and that was seventy-two hours back, two of us jawans had shared half a packet of biscuits. We need not just food rations but also field bandages and ammunition. The number of enemy soldiers is almost ten times compared to us.'

The effort of talking was too much for me and my speech started failing. I asked for water, but he refused as he did not want to give me anything without the consent of the doctor.

Then the doctor at the Regimental Aid Post (RAP) came and gave me glucose to drink. This brought back some life within me.

The doctor and the CO talked for some time. In between, the doctor gave me an injection and I lost consciousness completely. I did not know what was happening around me or where I was taken. I knew nothing.

Maybe during the night, I was taken down from the mountain. When they were taking off my boots, the right one could not be taken off. When they pulled at it hard, it pained a lot and I opened my eyes again. I told them that something was stuck in my foot.

Then they noticed that a piece of grenade was stuck in it, right up to my toe. They took it out and then took off the boot. I could not feel any of that.

I regained consciousness after three days and saw that I was in a hospital in Srinagar. There I came to know that our team had launched another attack and managed to hoist our tiranga on Tiger Hill. That is what I had been waiting to hear for so many days. My fellows had finally completed what we had started. It was a victory for the country and all of us in the Armed Forces.

After the victory on Tiger Hill, the Kargil War soon came to an end. A number of soldiers of the Indian Army had laid down their lives to retain the honour of the country. It was a great victory.

> *The first thing my heart felt and my mouth gave voice to was* – 'Jai Hind!'

36

A New Start

It was a new life for me at the hospital. After spending sixteen months on the hospital bed, I was finally discharged.

It was a long road to recovery and I spent months at the Base Hospital in Delhi, regaining my strength.

In August that year, when the gallantry awards were announced, I was told that Yogendra Singh from our Unit was being awarded the Param Vir Chakra, posthumously. I was happy that my friend Yogendra had won the highest military honour of the country. Then the next day, I was formally communicated by the Chief of the Army Staff that it was I who was being honoured with the Param Vir Chakra. My happiness knew no bounds. It seemed like god's kindness was showering all over me.

There was also some miscommunication when I was unconscious for three days at the hospital in Srinagar. My family read in the papers that Yogenda Singh Yadav from 18 Grenadiers was one of the soldiers who laid his life in the line of duty. That was a terrible time for my family, especially my wife who had been in the family only for a couple of months. But thankfully, facts came to light and they realised that it was my namesake who we had lost. While the pain of losing a fellow remained, my family felt immense gratitude in knowing that I was recovering.

When I was discharged from the hospital, I went to my Unit. It was the start of a new era, a new life. I went to IMA, Dehradun. I met people there and discussed a lot of ideas with them. I was invited to many colleges and gatherings, but I realized that I could not speak on the stage on such occasions. I had never attended such programmes. For the first time, I was taken from the hospital to the village where I was supposed to address ten thousand people.

My hands were trembling as I held the mic because I had never seen such a large gathering before. I had never faced a crowd earlier. Then I felt that this was a shortcoming which I would have to overcome. Maybe this was because of lack of education. I decided to pursue education further.

At that time, I had passed the class ten examination. I passed my class twelve examination and then, did my graduation. After that, I started attending small programmes and events more confidently.

I remember, I could speak for twenty minutes in Agra. After that, I slowly lost my inhibitions. I gained enough self-confidence to face people and keep my point of view before them. This happened because now I had words through which I could describe my experiences, ideas and insights. Earlier, I did not have the power to express myself.

I learned immensely by reading books and interacting with different people. My vocabulary improved and I tried using new words in my everyday conversations. In 2013, I took admission in B.Ed.

I continued going for programmes to schools and NGOs.

After completing B.Ed. my life changed totally. While pursuing my Bachelor's in Education from the Army Educational Corps Training College and Centre (AEC) in Panchmarhi in Madhya Pradesh, I had to help the teachers in making basic teaching charts, diagrams, lesson plans and took them to class to teach. I gained a lot of knowledge there and that boosted my self confidence.

Then I went to IIT Kanpur to conduct my first big public speaking event. I got a very good response there. People appreciated my speech and asked me questions. I was greatly satisfied that I could share my life experiences and learnings with such polished minds.

I also went to IIM, Ahmedabad. Then, went to IIM, Indore where I was feeling a bit hesitant to speak in front of so many people. All of them were brilliant and wanted to gain an in-depth knowledge of everything. I listened to their questions and replied as best as I could. I always ensured that positivity oozed out of my thoughts, which is a clear reflection of how I do things in life.

When I had gone to IIT Kanpur for the first time, a girl asked me a question which I could answer after a lot of deliberaton.

Army has always been a very transparent organisation and I answered the question, keeping that in mind.

She asked, 'Sir, if there is so much transparency, the person who runs the country, could run the army as well. Isn't it?'

I understood her question and said, 'You have asked the right question. You are talking about Dr APJ Abdul Kalam, isn't it? He could not make it through the SSB[10] examinations.' All the students looked at me to listen to what I was going to say.

I said, 'This is the gift of our Army to the nation, which gave the country a missile man.' She looked surprised and I said, 'The Army does not only look at someone's IQ, but several other factors before recruitment. Dr Kalam was exceptional in intelligence, but maybe there were other factors that led to this decision. Several key factors like performing under pressure, managing a team, carrying on with mental resilience for days and months make up for some factors. So while he was rejected by the Army, that failure became a driving force for him to focus on something different and he became the missile man. Today he is the President of India.'

There were several such situations that gave me immense exposure. I was given a new perspective and talking to these brilliant students gave me a new way of thinking which enhanced my life.

After that, I went to two or three universities in South India and also to the IITs of Delhi and Mumbai. I tried to tell the story of my life in a better and more effective way. People listened to me and appreciated what I said.

---

10. Service Selection Board.

The reason I am saying all this and the main reason behind writing this book is that you can be ordinary, but you can become a hero, if you have the right mindset to tackle difficult circumstances.

If we realize our shortcomings at the right time and start working on them, nothing is impossible. A sportsperson is nothing to start with, but with practice, he improves his skill and can even become a gold medallist one day.

The only condition is that a person must have the will power to do something good. This can be done by listening to positive ideas. You should have the ability to listen to people attentively. You can have a good vocabulary only if you are fond of reading books. You will have a treasure trove of knowledge. When you have both words and powerful ideas, you will have no inhibition in putting across your views. You will be able to put across your views effectively and connect directly with your audience.

The communication can be impactful only when the audience can connect with you. I was in Junior Leaders Academy for eight years. While I was there, around fifty-six thousand students studied there. There too, my interpersonal skills improved. This was because I met them everywhere, talked to them, discussed things with them – all this helped me to enhance my skills. This was the beginning of a new chapter in my life.

Today, after retiring from the Army, I have started on a new phase in life. I hope I can do something fruitful in this phase and contribute something meaningful to the society and my country.

37

POSTFACE CITATIONS

Several bravehearts laid their lives on the road to winning the Kargil War. While I salute the grit and passion of each one of them and bow down in respect, there were a select few who were recognized for their extraordinary valour in the face of all odds.

The following soldiers received the highest gallantry awards for their exemplary bravery. This section gives details of action they were heading and how they valiantly laid their lives for Mother India.

Award	Rank	Name	Unit
Param Vir Chakra	Grenadier	Yogendra Singh Yadav	18 Grenadiers
Param Vir Chakra	Lieutenant	Manoj Kumar Pandey	1/11 Gorkha Rifles
Param Vir Chakra	Captain	Vikram Batra	13 JAK Rifles

Award	Rank	Name	Unit
Param Vir Chakra	Rifleman	Sanjay Kumar	13 JAK Rifles
Mahavir Chakra	Captain	Anuj Nayyar	17 Jat
Mahavir Chakra	Major	Rajesh Singh Adhikari	18 Grenadiers
Mahavir Chakra	Captain	Gurjinder Singh Suri	12 Bihar
Mahavir Chakra	Naik	Digendra Kumar	2 Rajputana Rifles
Mahavir Chakra	Naik	Imliakum Ao	2 Naga
Mahavir Chakra	Captain	Keishing Clifford Nongrum	2 JAK LI
Mahavir Chakra	Captain	Neikezhakuo Kenguruse	2 Rajputana Rifles
Mahavir Chakra	Major	Padmapani Acharya	2 Rajputana Rifles
Mahavir Chakra	Major	Sonam Wangchuk	Ladakh Scouts
Mahavir Chakra	Major	Vivek Gupta	2 Rajputana Rifles
Mahavir Chakra	Lieutenant	Balwan Singh	18 Grenadiers
Vir Chakra	Lieutenant Colonel	R Vishwanathan	18 Grenadiers
Vir Chakra	L/HAV	Ram Kumar	18 Grenadiers

Some of the above-mentioned heroes appear in the autobiography. Since Capt. (Hony) Yogendra Singh Yadav interacted with them first-hand in the line of his duty, the citations for their gallantry awards are reproduced in the following pages.

YOGENDRA SINGH YADAV, 18 GRENADIERS

PARAM VIR CHAKRA

Grenadier Yogendra Singh Yadav was part of the leading team of Ghatak Platoon tasked to capture Tiger Hill on the night of 3/4 July 1999. The approach to the top was steep, snow bound and rocky. Grenadier Yogendra Singh Yadav, unmindful of the risk involved, volunteered to be in the lead and fixed rope of his team to climb up. On seeing the team, the enemy opened intense automatic grenade, rocket and artillery fire killing the commander and two of his colleagues and the platoon was stalled. Realising the gravity of the situation, Grenadier Yadav crawled up to the enemy position to silence it and in the process sustained multiple injuries. Unmindful of his injuries and in the hail of enemy bullets, Grenadier Yadav continued climbing towards the enemy positions. Lobbing grenades and continuously firing from his weapon, he killed four enemy soldiers in close combat and silenced the automatic fire. Despite multiple injuries, he refused to be evacuated and continued the charge. Inspired by his gallant act, the platoon charged on to the other positions with renewed punch and captured Tiger Hill Top.

Grenadier Yogendra Singh Yadav displayed the most conspicuous courage, indomitable gallantry, grit and determination under extreme adverse circumstances.

MAJOR RAJESH SINGH ADHIKARI, 18 GRENADIERS

MAHA VIR CHAKRA

On 30 May 1999, as a part of battalion operation to capture the Tololing feature, Major Rajesh Singh Adhikari was tasked to secure the initial foothold by capturing its forward spur where the enemy held a strong position. The enemy position was located in a treacherous mountainous terrain covered with snow at a height of about 15,000 feet. While Major Adhikari was leading his company towards the objective, he was fired at from two mutually supporting enemy positions with Universal machine guns. The officer immediately directed the rocket launcher detachment to engage the enemy position and killed two enemy soldiers in close quarter combat. Thereafter, the officer, displaying presence of mind under heavy fire, ordered his medium machine gun detachment to take position behind a rocky feature and engage the enemy. The assault party continued to inch their way up. While so advancing forward, Major Adhikari suffered grievous bullet injuries, yet he continued to direct his sub-unit. Refusing to be evacuated, then he charged at the second enemy position and killed

one more occupant, thus capturing the second position at Tololing which later facilitated capture of Point 4590. However later he succumbed to his injuries.

Major Rajesh Singh Adhikari displayed exceptional valour, outstanding leadership in the presence of the enemy and laid down his life in the highest traditions of the Indian Army.

LIEUTENANT BALWAN SINGH
18 GRENADIERS

MAHA VIR CHAKRA

On 03 July 1999 Lieutenant Balwan Singh with his Ghatak platoon was tasked to assault the 'Tiger Hill Top' from the North Eastern direction as part of a multi pronged attack. The route to the objective situated at a height of 16,500 feet was snowbound and interspersed with crevasses and sheer falls. The officer, with just three months service, set about his task with single-minded determination. The team led and exhorted by him, moved for over twelve hours along a very difficult and precarious route and under intense artillery shelling to reach the designated spur.

This move took the enemy by complete surprise as his team used cliff assault mountaineering equipment to reach the top with stealth. On seeing the Ghataks, the enemy panicked and in a desperate firefight attempted to repulse the Ghataks. In the ensuing firefight, Lieutenant Balwan Singh was himself seriously injured. However his resolve to finish the enemy remained unshaken. He refused to be evacuated and unmindful of his injury, moved swiftly to encircle the enemy and engaged them in close combat and single handedly killed four enemy

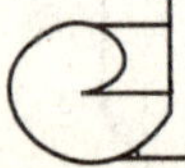

soldiers. The remaining enemy personnel opted to flee rather than face the fury of the fierce officer. His inspirational leadership, conspicuous courage and bravery were instrumental in the capture of Tiger Hill, which was operationally one of the most important objectives in the Dras sector.

LT COL RAMAKRISHNAN VISHWANATHAN 18 GRENADIERS

VIR CHAKRA

During 'Operation Vijay', Lieutenant Colonel Ramakrishnan Vishwanathan was the Second-in-Command of 18 Grenadiers, which was conducting operations in the Tololing area of Drass sector. He displayed rare valour in closing in on enemy positions under prohibitive enemy automatic fire and intense artillery shelling, thus taking the enemy by complete surprise along a very difficult approach and terrain at an altitude ofover 15,000 feet. During the attack, Lieutenant Colonel Vishwanathan sustained multiple gunshot wounds. In spite of being severely injured he refused to be evacuated and exhorted his troops to press on further. He charged through enemy defences destroying three enemy positions and eliminated four intruders single-handedly in a close hand-to-hand combat. Due to his efforts, the battalion could secure a foothold on the enemy location which later facilitated capture of Point 4590.

Though Second-in-Command of his unit, Lieutenant Colonel Ramakrishnan Vishwanathan disregarded his seniority and preferred being

where his men were fighting: and led from the front during assaults on well-fortified enemy positions in Tololing. He however succumbed to his injuries making the supreme sacrifice for the nation in the best traditions of the Indian Army.

List of Acronyms

CHM – Company Havaldar Major
EME – Electronics And Mechanical Engineers
JCO – Junior Commissioned Officer
LMG – Light Machine Gun
LoC – Line of Control
PT – Physical Training
RAP – Regimental Aid Post
SAM – Surface To Air Missile
SSC – Service Selection Board
TC – Training Company
UMG – Universal Machine Gun